VAN WOLVERT[ON]

WORDPERFECT® 6.0

Easy Directions for Immediate Results

VAN WOLVERTON & JIM MEADE

RANDOM HOUSE
ELECTRONIC PUBLISHING

New York

Van Wolverton's Guide to WordPerfect 6.0

Published in the United States by Random House, Inc., New York, and simultaneously in Canada by Random House of Canada Limited.

Manufactured in the United States of America

First Edition

ISBN: 0-679-73915-7

New York, Toronto, London, Sydney, Auckland

Dedication

In memory of my father,
whose words, at times,
were perfect.

J.G.M.

Acknowledgments

We're indebted to our agent, Claudette Moore, for getting us together with each other and with the people at Random House. We thank Lesa Carter at WordPerfect for providing pre-release software so that our book could come out when WordPerfect 6.0 did, and the Random House editing and production staff for bringing the book from manuscript to finished book. Above all, we thank our wives and families.

CONTENTS

INTRODUCTION

In an ideal world, sitting down with your new copy of WordPerfect 6.0 would be like flipping on the switch on a new color television. You wouldn't have to learn anything, and a whole world of possibilities would appear. With that television, you might take a moment here and there to pick up something new about pushing the buttons on the remote control or adjusting the color, but you wouldn't think of that as learning. You'd just take on the knack for this or that as you enjoyed your movies, sports, and soaps. You might even end up as a quite sophisticated color television user, but you wouldn't pause to congratulate yourself on that; you'd just watch televsion.

The goal of this guide is to provide you with such an ideal world with WordPerfect. Nobody except a training professional really aspires to be a sophisticated WordPerfect user for its own sake. People want to get something done with WordPerfect, the faster the better, while paying as little attention to WordPerfect itself as possible.

How the Book Works

How does this book move toward that ideal? Mainly, it gets you doing things, with a minimum of talk beforehand and a minimum of reflection afterwards. It tells you what you're going to do, has you do it, then mentions briefly that you've done it.

Here you don't find out about terminology for its own sake. You don't have to ascertain what the messages in various parts of the screen tell you (until the time comes up, later, that you actually refer to them.) And you don't find out right away about all the alternative ways to do anything. A surprising level of accomplishment can sneak up on you when you use a word processor to do things without thinking much about how to use it to do things.

What You Find Here

After the briefest of introductions to word processing and your computer, you start out using your word processor like a typewriter. You type a few simple things, make minor corrections, and transfer your typed work onto paper. Probably many WordPerfect users don't go much further than that.

Here, though, you slide from doing some typing to doing a little bit more, like a hiker who just wants to see what's around one more twist in the trail. You move into some of the special capabilities waiting at your fingertips—cut and paste, search and replace, spell checking, using an electronic Thesaurus, and having the computer check your grammar.

From there you see how to dress up your text and the appearance of the page. Then, when you can dress it up that far, you go a little further and add tables, even pictures.

Once you can do so much with WordPerfect, you're ready to put WordPerfect to the test a bit and ask it to work the way you work. You see how to change the screen colors, change the messages on the screen, things like that. Then, as a finale, you see how to automate your work by collecting multiple steps into a single step (a macro) and by creating a personalized mass mailing.

At this point, you've come a long way with little effort, and you're a quite proficient WordPerfect user.

PART I

GETTING YOURSELF CLICKING AWAY

Often there's no better way to get started than to just get started. WordPerfect is a tool, and you're to be its master. Part 1 gets you started, first, by introducing you to word processing and discussing what your computer has to do with it all. In the second chapter it shows you how to use WordPerfect as barely more than an ordinary typewriter for typing text, changing it, and printing it. Just as you're beginning to gather momentum, Chapter 3 introduces some of the wonders of WordPerfect; you use it to center text automatically, cut and paste text (with no mess), search for something and replace it, find synonyms, check spelling, and even check grammar.

CHAPTER

I

WHAT IT MEANS TO
PROCESS WORDS

No doubt you've heard that WordPerfect is a "word processor," but what is a word processor anyway, and what does that mean for you as you use one? Other processors are easy enough to understand. A food processor chops carrots in various, often creative ways at astonishing speeds. It comes with several different knives, but you very well may end up using just one or two. It can get jammed, but you just stop it and pull out some of the extra carrots to fix it.

A word processor, by analogy, slices *words* at astonishing speeds, in ways that you might not do on your own. It can do all kinds of things, but most of the time you probably do only a few of them. It can stall, but if you get back to basics you'll be all right.

Keyboard, Monitor, and Printer

Your computer running WordPerfect doesn't look much like the old style word processor: a typewriter. The typewriter comes all in one piece, but your computer has four or five pieces, as you can see in Figure 1-1. There's a *keyboard* where you type things; there's a *monitor* where you see what you're typing (instead of seeing it on a piece of paper); there may be a hand-held device called a *mouse* right next to the keyboard; there's a *printer* that has paper in it; and there's a box with a couple slots in the front that holds the mysteries of your computer itself.

The computer keyboard is just like a typewriter keyboard; you press the keys to indicate the letters you want to type. The mouse also takes instructions from your fingers to the computer, but it has just two keys; you move the mouse to point at things on the screen, then press one of the keys.

The monitor does what the piece of paper in a typewriter does: It shows you what you've typed. The printer allows you to transfer words from the screen into words in the familiar form you've seen with typewriters—printed form.

The box with the slots in it contains the computer, where all the "processing" goes on that allows the word processor to earn its name. On a typewriter you press a key like the "b" key, and you see a "b" on the screen, but you don't type in commands and expect the typewriter to follow them. On the word processor, you can press a "b" and see a "b," but you can also type in all kinds of commands and have it carry them out. The computer is to a typewriter what a telephone is to shouting over the back fence.

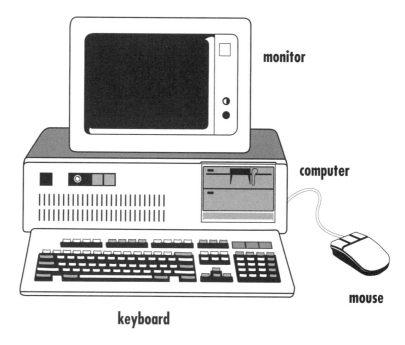

Figure 1-1 The computer has a few distinct parts.

WordPerfect Turns a Computer Into a Word Processor

What is the role of WordPerfect with your computer? A computer, by itself, is enormous, sleeping potential. To turn the computer into something useful, you need programs that apply that potential of the computer to certain everyday capabilities, such as word processing. You can have many programs on your computer at the same time, such as a spreadsheet for working with numbers, a graphics program for doing charts, a tax program, games, and more. But word processing is the most common use of a computer, and WordPerfect is the most widely used word processing program. When you first start the computer you have to tell it which program you want to use; WordPerfect doesn't just start automatically.

What MS-DOS Has to Do with It

MS-DOS, another term you've probably encountered already, is software inside the computer that makes WordPerfect and your other programs work successfully with the computer itself. DOS, you could say, is the traffic cop who sends instructions from WordPerfect to the computer and from the computer back to WordPerfect. Much of the time, you can work with WordPerfect without thinking much about that traffic cop doing his work in the background. You do work directly in DOS when you start WordPerfect or any of your other programs; and sometimes you may choose to use DOS itself rather than WordPerfect for doing things like making extra copies of documents you have created or deleting documents you no longer need.

Memory and Storage, and Why it Matters

When you type on a typewriter, your words appear on the page. They're permanent, unless you happen to lose the printed page; but when you type into a computer and see your words on the screen, those words aren't yet permanent. They're in the computer's memory, but it's only a short-term memory. If you turn the computer off, you lose the words altogether. To keep from losing them, you have to transfer them from memory to permanent storage on the computer's hard disk. The disk is inside the computer, and you may never even see it. Putting your work onto it (using the Save command, described shortly) is like taking a photograph of an important moment instead of trying to carry the memory of it inside your head.

Hard Disks and Floppy Disks, and Why That Matters

Though you store your files permanently on a hard disk, you also use another type of disk—floppy disks—which you slide in and out of those slots on the front of the computer. You use floppy disks to put programs into the computer in the first place, and you also use them to make backup copies of the work on your hard drive.

You certainly don't have to be an expert in hardware and software to use your word processor on your computer. It helps to know why you do some of the things you do such as typing a command at the DOS prompt to get started, giving special commands to send your work to a printer, and (above all) saving work to disk even though you can see perfectly well that it's already up there on the screen. Knowing this much, you're ready to get that word processor going and see some of the fancy, electronic ways it can slice your words for you.

CHAPTER

2

USING WORDPERFECT LIKE
A HOT TYPEWRITER

Some people, accustomed to using typewriters in the past, feel somewhat apologetic about using their high-powered word processor only to speed up doing the same thing they did on the typewriter—namely, getting words onto paper in presentable form. It's like being ashamed of using the food processor just to grate cheese instead of to full prepare catered meals. But actually, in this workaday world, most of what anyone does with a word processor is typing, and using it like a typewriter in itself amounts to quite a lot.

Even when using the word processor as a typewriter, you type faster than on a typewriter, make your changes easier, and produce better looking documents. Besides, it's just natural to pick up some of WordPerfect's word processing capabilities without even thinking about it as you go along. There is nothing wrong, then, with using WordPerfect the way you always used your typewriter.

Starting Up

Starting up WordPerfect is a matter of typing a single, short command:

1. Flip the switch to turn on the computer. You'll see the DOS prompt (usually *C:\>*), and a small blinking line right after it, called a *cursor*. When you type, letters appear where the cursor is.

2. Type WP and press Enter. You'll hear some purring, see a WordPerfect 6.0 copyright screen, and then see a blank screen like the one in Figure 2-1. You're ready to start typing.

Typing Something

Getting words onto the screen really is no different from getting them onto the page with a typewriter. Put your fingers on the keyboard and let fly. Type this:

```
The television promotional campaign has been
surprisingly successful. Get ready for a major
onslaught! Specifics will follow.
```

When you come to the end of the line, don't press Enter or Return as you would with a typewriter. Words flow over to the next line automatically (already a major advantage to using a word processor instead of a typewriter.) Press Enter only at the end of a paragraph. Try it:

1. Press Enter twice after what you just typed.

2. Type this:

```
Mr. Babcock has asked me to commend all of you for
running the kind of efficient operation that helps
such advertising to succeed.
```

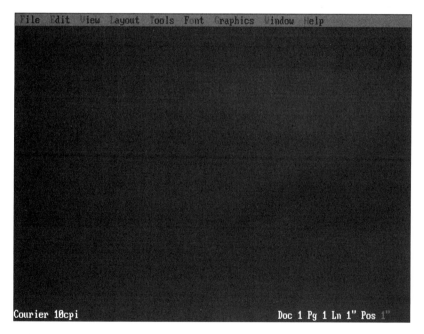

Figure 2-1 The Initial WordPerfect Screen.

Figure 2-2 shows the screen with these two paragraphs on it. The characters on the keyboard, the Enter key, and the space bar (the main keys anyone uses when word processing) work the same as on a keyboard. Making changes is similar, too, except that you don't have to fool with liquid white out.

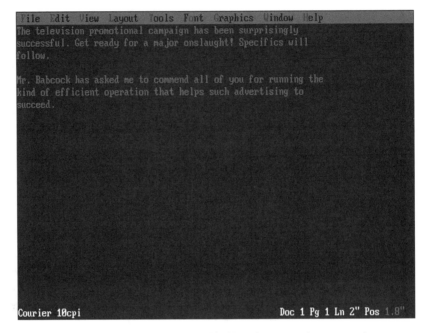

Figure 2-2 You type in paragraphs like these much as you do on a typewriter.

Changing Things Without Erasers and White Out

If word processors did nothing more than make it much easier to make changes, they'd already be worth the purchase price. You can use the same keys you used on a typewriter to make changes, or you can use some additional keys that make things a little faster and easier.

Making Changes the Old Typewriter Way

If you wanted, you could just make changes in word processing the way you always did with the typewriter. The Backspace key, old reliable on a typewriter, does the trick on a word processor, too.

Deleting with the Backspace Key Try making a change now:

1. Press the Backspace key (a left facing arrow, just next to the +/= key on the top row of your keyboard) eight times to delete the word *succeed* and the period after it.

2. Type in the replacement phrase `win people over` and follow it with a period.

Moving with the Arrow Keys When you type in WordPerfect, the cursor makes space for new words if you type them in front of words that are already there. Use the arrow keys to move the cursor in front of some text, then try it:

1. Press the up arrow key once and the left arrow key several times so that the cursor is under the e at the start of *efficient.* (There are two sets of arrow keys. One set, between the letter keyboard on the left and the set of number keys on the right, just works as direction keys and doesn't double as anything else. Use that one.)

2. Type `strong,` in front of the word *efficient* so that the phrase now reads *strong, efficient operation.* The new text doesn't go on top of the old text as it would on a typewriter; in this electronic world it can push the existing text away in front of itself.

Typing Over Old Text You can, though, type over existing text if you wish:

1. Use the arrow keys to put the cursor under the *c* in *commend* in the first line of the second paragraph.

2. Press the key labeled *Insert,* just above the arrows keys and to the right of the Backspace key. The words *Courier 10cpi* in the lower left of the screen change to *Typeover.*

3. Type `praise.` The characters replace the characters in *commend.*

4. Press Insert again to leave Typeover Mode and go back to Insert Mode, where the new words don't type over existing words.

Making Changes the Electronic Way

The additional editing keys for the word processor are just as straightforward as the trusty old Backspace key, and let you do things just not possible with a typewriter. Here's where you start getting into the *processing* part of word processing.

Deleting with the Del Key   In the previous example where you type over characters, you still have a character to get rid of—the *d* left from the end of *commend*. You can use the Del key:

Check the right side of the top row of the keyboard to make sure the green light isn't on under Num Lock. Then press the Del key once (on the lower right of the small keypad, between the Ins and Enter keys.) The unwanted *d* goes away.

Holding Down Keys to Repeat Them   You can also hold down any key to have it repeat:

Press the right arrow key once to put the cursor under the *a* in *all,* then hold down Del. WordPerfect gobbles up several words. Hold down Del until you've gobbled up all the rest of the words in the paragraph.

"You Mean, I Can Get It Back?" Esc Key

It's nice that it's so easy to delete text, but what if you change your mind? WordPerfect is forgiving:

1. Press Esc (the key off by itself on the top left, with Esc on it.) A box appears with Undelete at the top. See Figure 2-3.

2. Type r to choose Restore. WordPerfect puts back the text you just deleted.

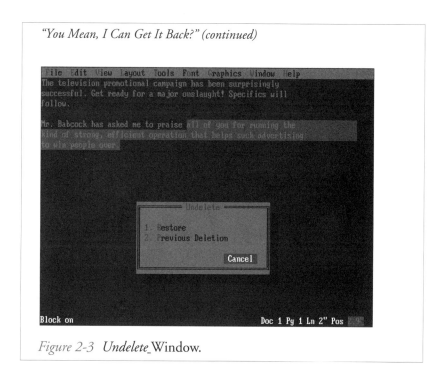

"You Mean, I Can Get It Back?" (continued)

Figure 2-3 Undelete Window.

Making Sure the Computer Remembers

As you write your text, you don't want to lose the benefits of your creativity, but text you see on the screen isn't permanently stored until you issue a command to do that. Here the similarities to a typewriter disappear, and the power of the computer steps in—you can store many pages of text in a small space on the computer's hard disk.

Opening a Menu

The words across the very top of the screen are the menus that contain the commands you use to tell WordPerfect what to do. You need one of those commands in the File menu to store the text on the screen permanently on your hard disk:

1. Hold down the Alt key (on the bottom row of the keyboard, labeled *Alt*) and, as you keep it down, press f to display the

commands in the File menu. The File menu drops down showing the commands it contains. As Figure 2-4 shows, each command in the menu has one letter that is darker or in a different color. You can use that key to choose the command.

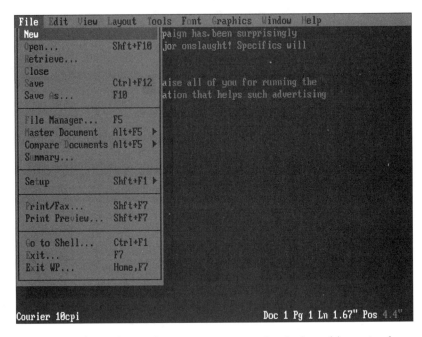

Figure 2-4 To choose from a menu, press the darkened letter in the command you want.

2. Press s. A window appears called Save Document 1 (see Figure 2-5). You're ready to save the document to disk.

Typing a Name

The cursor is already in the right position in the new window:

Type the name promo and press Enter. A message flashes by quickly saying that you've saved the file, and you go back into the document. The document is permanent, and you can now see its name in the bottom left of the screen along with some letters in front of it that tell you its location in DOS.

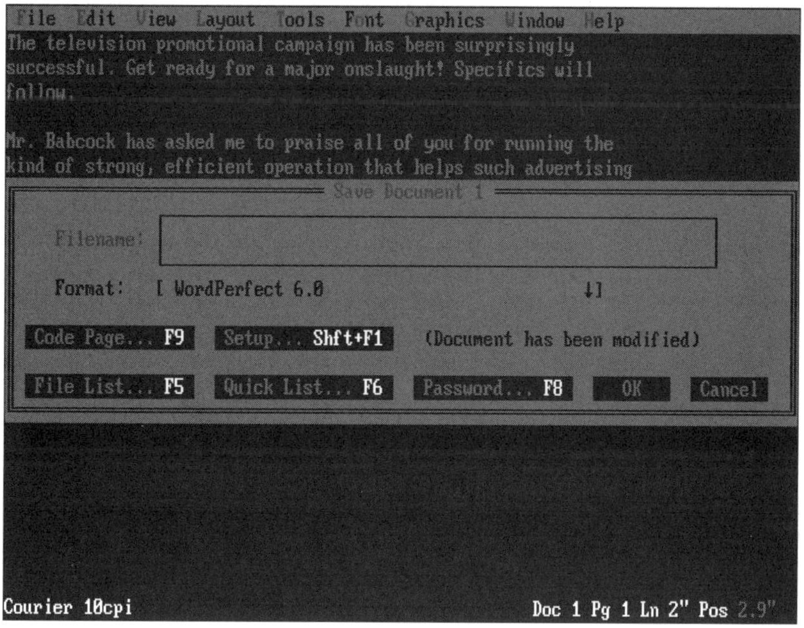

Figure 2-5 Use this window to save a document to disk.

Though most of us end up learning the lesson the hard way by losing our work now and then, saving your text to disk is about the best habit you can get into as you use your word processor. If you accidentally close a file, the power fails, or your system stops working for any reason, you lose all the work you've done since the last time you saved.

Once you've named the file, saving is even easier than it was the first time. Try saving the file again now that it has a name:

1. Press Alt+f to display the File menu. (When you see a the command typed this way, with a plus sign in the middle, it means hold down the first key while you press the second.)

2. Press s to save the file. WordPerfect saves the file to disk without asking you to assign a name.

Having made certain that you won't lose your work accidentally, you can get back to editing it.

Using Shortcuts in Moving Around

Any time you're not sure how to move from one place to another, you can always just use the arrow keys, but there are faster ways. Suppose, for instance, you wanted to go to the top of the file:

1. Press the Home key twice, then the up arrow. The cursor goes to the top of the document. That's not much easier than pressing the up arrow key right now when you have just a couple paragraphs, but it becomes most useful as you write documents that are several pages long.

2. Check to make sure the word *Typeover* isn't in the bottom left of the screen, then type `Memorandum: To Department Heads`, and press Enter twice.

Try moving forward a word at a time:

1. Hold down the Ctrl key (bottom left of the keyboard) and press the right arrow key once. The cursor moves right a whole word at once.

2. Type the word `new` in front of *television*.

3. Hold down Ctrl and press the down arrow to move to the start of the next paragraph.

4. Type `our` in front of *Mr. Babcock*.

5. Save the document (type Alt+f, then s).

At first you won't remember these key combinations for moving around, and you won't need them all. But using a few of them can make it easy to get where you want quickly.

Mice Scurry Around Fast

If you have a mouse, you don't have to bother to learn key combinations for getting around in the document or for opening menus. To put the cursor anywhere on the screen, slide the mouse around on the desktop until the colored block on the screen (the mouse pointer) is in the position you want, then click the mouse once. The cursor moves to that

> *Mice Scurry Around Fast (continued)*
>
> spot, and you can type.
>
> To choose any command from the menus, just put the mouse pointer on top of the command and click.
>
> Don't worry, by the way, if you don't see the mouse pointer until you need it. WordPerfect feels that if you're not using the mouse pointer it'll just confuse you to have it there on the screen; so as soon as you type something on the keyboard, the mouse pointer disappears. Just move the mouse slightly, and it'll come back.

Printing Electronic Words on Good Old Paper

Once you have words on your screen, even if you've stored them on your disk, you still can't shove them into an envelope and carry them over to your colleagues at the office. In the end, having enjoyed all the speed and cleanliness of typing on the screen instead of on paper, you often end up putting the words on paper.

To print, again use the menus and commands as you did to save:

1. Press Alt+f to display the File menu.

2. Press p. A *Print/Fax* window opens, shown in Figure 2-6.

3. Press Enter. The printer starts printing your WordPerfect document. If nothing prints, make sure the printer is turned on and has paper in it.

Putting WordPerfect Away At Night

Once you've printed the document, you may have the final product you had in mind. However, the document is still there on the screen.

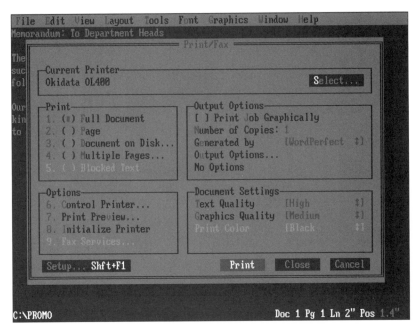

Figure 2-6 You see this window when you choose *Print* from the
File menu.

Closing the Document

Here's how to close a document once you don't want to work with
it any longer. (It's still saved on your disk so if you want it again,
you can get it):

1. Press Alt+f.

2. Press e. A window pops up and asks if you want to save the
   document. WordPerfect always tries to make its best guess as
   to your answer. If you haven't changed the document since
   the last time you used it, *No* is already highlighted, as in this
   case (see Figure 2-7).

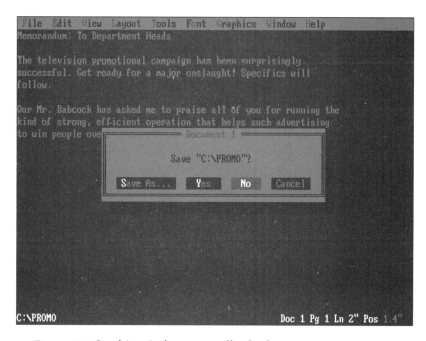

Figure 2-7 In this window you tell whether or not you want to save the document again before you leave it.

3. Press Enter.

WordPerfect then asks if you want to Exit WordPerfect altogether. *No* is already highlighted.

4. Press Enter. You return to WordPerfect, but the document isn't on the screen any longer.

Getting Out of WordPerfect

Eventually the time comes when you do want to close down WordPerfect. Again you use the File menu:

1. Press Alt+, then x to choose Exit from the File menu. The Exit WordPerfect window comes up, and *Exit* is already highlighted.

2. Press Enter.

WordPerfect goes off the screen, and you see the DOS prompt where you began.

Even when you plan to do just the most simple things with your word processor, then, you begin to have a lot of power at your fingertips. You can chop away whole passages at the press of a couple keys and replace them without ever having to roll a fresh piece of paper into the typewriter. You've already used your word processor to do what you want. The word processor can do some amazing things that a typewriter can't do, even in its wildest dreams. You're ready to try some of these things out in the next chapter.

CHAPTER

3

DOING SOME THINGS TYPEWRITERS JUST DON'T DO

Using WordPerfect as a hot typewriter is just the beginning. Take simple things everybody does, like moving text around; they're a big deal on a typewriter. Lots of times it's easier just to type a page over than to find a way to move a few words from one part of the page to another. Anyway, the typewriter isn't some Rube Goldberg invention with scissors and glue inside itself. Moving words is easy on the word processor, though, and WordPerfect does have "scissors and glue" inside itself (except they're electronic and you can't cut yourself on them or get sticky.)

Go a step further. How could a typewriter ever have a Thesaurus inside itself, look up words for you, and offer you alternatives? The Thesaurus would jam up the typewriter keys, and the typewriter can't see to look up words anyway. WordPerfect does have an electronic Thesaurus inside itself, and a spelling checker, even a grammar checker. In this chapter you look at some of the electronic wizardry you can do on your word processor and see that it's a lot easier than what you used to do by hand.

Getting Your Essay Back

Putting your document away in WordPerfect as you did in the last chapter is a little like throwing a rock into the ocean; your hard drive has room for thousands of documents like that one. Here's how to get it back once you've put it away:

1. Type WP at the DOS prompt to start WordPerfect.

2. To choose *Open* from the File menu, press Alt+f, then press the down arrow once to highlight *Open,* and press Enter. The Open Document window opens, Figure 3-1.

3. In the box next to *Filename:,* where the cursor is flashing, type in Promo, the name of the document, and press Enter. The document comes back onto the screen.

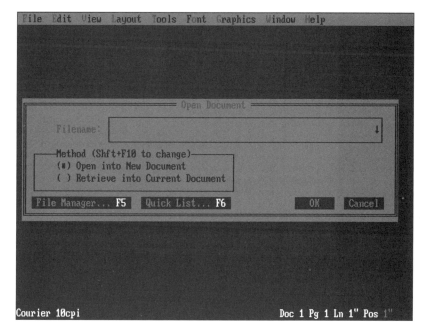

Figure 3-1 Use this Window to find a document you've saved before.

"I Forgot What I Named It."

It's easy to forget what you named something, and as you create more and more documents it becomes almost impossible to remember. WordPerfect includes a feature called the File Manager that lets you display the names of files stored on your hard disk. Suppose you wanted to find *Promo* but didn't remember its name:

1. Follow steps 1 to 3 under "Getting Your Essay Back" to get to the Open Document window.

2. Press the F5 key (a *Function Key,* in the very top row of the keyboard). A window opens that says *Specify File Manager List.*

"I Forgot What I Named It." (continued)

3. Press Enter without changing anything. The *File Manager* opens, which lists all the files on your hard drive by name (not just your WordPerfect documents.)

Because you've already opened *Promo,* you don't need to open it again, so go to step 4 here to close the File Manager. If you were looking for a file you'd forgotten the name of, you'd use the arrow keys to highlight the name of the file you wanted, then press Enter.

4. Press Esc twice to close the File Manager without using it and get back to the document.

Selecting the Text to Work With

When you want to do something with some text, you first select the text, then tell WordPerfect what to do. You select text using what WordPerfect refers to as *blocking.* For example, to select all the text in the line *Memorandum: To Department Heads:*

1. Be sure the cursor is beneath the *M* in *Memorandum.*

2. Press Alt+e to display the Edit menu, shown in Figure 3-2.

3. Highlight *Block,* and press Enter. The message in the bottom left of the screen now says *Block on.*

4. Press and hold down the right arrow key to highlight all the text in the line. Stop right after the *s* in *Heads.* (If you go too far, use the left arrow key to go back until you've highlighted just the words.)

Having told WordPerfect which text to work with, you're ready to change it.

Centering a Line

To center a line on a typewriter, you usually have to do some figuring about the size of the page and the size of the line you want to center. WordPerfect does all that for you:

1. With the line you want to work with selected, press Alt+l to open the Layout menu.

2. Press l to open the *Line Format* window (Figure 3-3.)

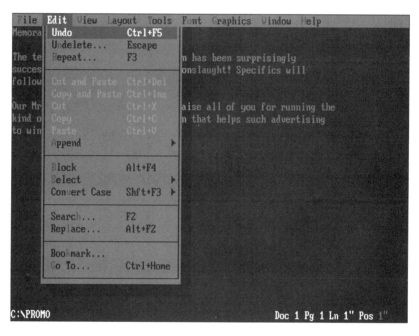

Figure 3-2 Use the Edit menu to work with text in various ways.

3. Press the Tab key three times to move the cursor to the box labeled *Justification*.

4. Press the Space bar to move the highlight to *Left*.

Notice that now each command in the Justification box has a dark letter in it; you can press that letter to choose the command.

5. Press c. A small box appears in the parentheses before Center.

6. Press Enter. WordPerfect centers the selected text.

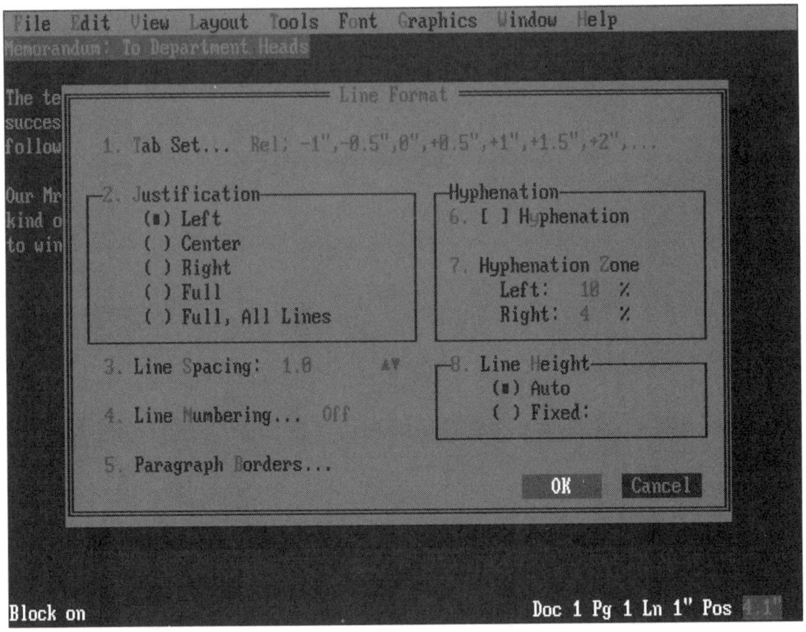

Figure 3-3 Use this window to format a line in various ways.

Changing Case

You can perform all kinds of wonders with your text by first indicating which text you want to work with, then choosing commands from menus.

To change all letters to uppercase, for example, choose the Case command from the Edit menu:

1. Select the first line, as your did when you centered the line.

2. Choose *Convert Case* from the Edit menu. A submenu opens for you to say which case you want to choose (see Figure 3-4). (The small triangle at the end of the menu line tells you there's another menu.)

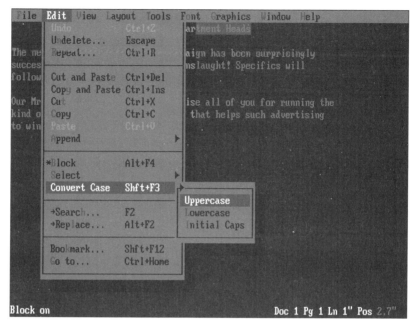

Figure 3-4 Use the submenu to say which case you want.

3. Make sure that *Upper* is highlighted.

Cutting and Pasting (Without Getting Your Fingers Sticky)

When you cut and paste text on a typewriter, the page never seems to look right after you're done; you usually have to retype it. Besides, scissors have a way of getting lost, and paste tends to dry up just when you need it most. When you cut and paste electronically, though, you face none of these problems.

Saving a Fresh Copy of a Document

First, save a copy of the current document under another name, so that the first version stays intact as you work on the second. You don't have to do this step to use cut and paste; it's just an easy way to experiment with a document while keeping the original intact in case you decide to go back to it:

1. Choose the Save As command from the File menu by pressing Alt+f, then a.

2. In the *Save Document 1* window, press End to move the cursor to the end of *C:\PROMO.*

3. Type 1, so that the new name is *C:\PROMO1,* and press Enter.

You're now working in a fresh copy of the same document you had before; the original is stored safely on your disk.

Cutting from One Place and Pasting to Another

Cutting text from one place and pasting it to another is easier, faster, and cleaner than on a typewriter. You block out text, then issue commands. The rest happens electronically, and instantaneously.

Using Key Combinations Instead of Menus   You used the menu to select text last time, but you can do it faster by just pressing certain keys and bypassing the menus:

1. You can mark the start of a block by pressing Alt+F4. Put the cursor under the *G* at the start of the second sentence in the first paragraph, and press Alt+F4.

2. To mark the text, move the cursor to the first letter of the next sentence, so that you've highlighted the exclamation point at the end of the sentence and the space after it.

You can start many WordPerfect commands by pressing combinations of keys instead of choosing the command from a menu. To find out what key combination to use for any given command, look at the menu (see Figure 3-2). You'll soon remember key combinations for commands you use often without having to refer to the menu.

Now that you've selected the text you're ready to cut it:

1. Press Alt+e to open the Edit menu, then press e for Cut and Paste. The highlighted text disappears from the page, but it's not gone. It's stored and waiting for the next step.

2. Press Home, Home, down arrow to move to the end of the document, and press the space bar once to position the text where you want to put it.

3. Choose Paste from the Edit menu by pressing Alt+e, then p. WordPerfect pastes the text at the end of the document.

4. Press Alt+f, then s to save the changed document.

"Hey, I Lost That Stuff I Was Pasting!"

It's a good idea to paste something right away after you cut it. When you cut or copy text, WordPerfect keeps it in an area of memory called the *Clipboard;* but it can only keep one thing in there at a time. Whatever you put in the Clipboard stays there only until you put something else in there; then whatever was in there before goes away.

Copying While Keeping the Original in Place

Typewriters don't give you the option of leaving the original text in place when you copy to another position, but word processors do. *Copying* is useful for addresses, lists, technical information, and much else. First, type some additional text at the end of the current document:

> Press End to go to the end of the line you just pasted in. Press Enter twice after the exclamation point, then type the following words, pressing Enter after each line:

```
We'll be starting campaigns in these places:

Chicago

Dallas

Los Angeles

New York

Portland
```

```
Sioux City
```

2. Save the document.

Now do the steps in the next section, *The Trick to Copying to Another Document,* to get a second document open along with this one.

Using Windows (The Trick to Copying to Another Document)

You've typed the list in one place, but suppose you wanted to copy it into a second document. You can keep the first one open and open a second one. (In fact, you can have up to nine documents open at once and switch among all of them, but for now you're just opening two.):

1. The New command in the File menu opens a new document. Press Alt+f, then n to open a document in a second window. As Figure 3-5 shows, the new document is blank and says *Doc 2* at the lower right.

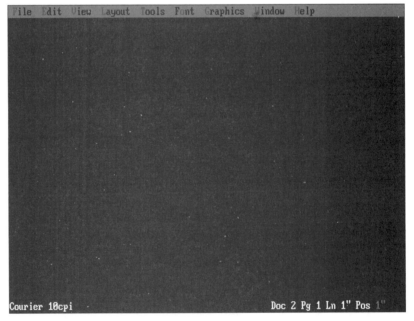

Figure 3-5 New, blank window.

2. So you can see both documents at the same time, press Alt+w, then t for *Tile.* The Tile command displays windows side-by-side, so each window takes up half the screen (see Figure 3-6).

3. The Shift+F3 key combination moves you from one window to the next. Press Shift+F3 to move back to the first window. You can tell which one you're in, because it has a double border around it.

Now, with the additional text in the document and a second window open, you're ready to copy from one document to another:

1. Put the cursor under the *C* in *Chicago,* press Alt+F4, then press the down arrow key five times to select the list of cities.

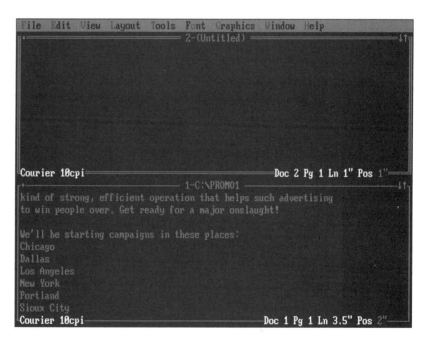

Figure 3-6 You can set up two documents so you can see them both on the screen.

2. Choose *Copy* from the Edit menu to copy the text to the clipboard. Notice that the highlighting disappears but this

time the text stays where it was in the original document. (When you cut the text, it disappeared).

3. Press Shift+F3 to move to the second document.

4. Choose Paste from the Edit menu to paste the list into the second window. Figure 3-7 shows what you get.

5. You can use keystrokes instead of the menus. Press F7 to exit the second window. The window was just for the example, so choose *No* from the window asking if you want to save it, then choose *Yes* to the message asking if you want to exit without saving your changes.

6. To have the window that's still open take up the full screen again, press Alt+w, then m to *Maximize* it.

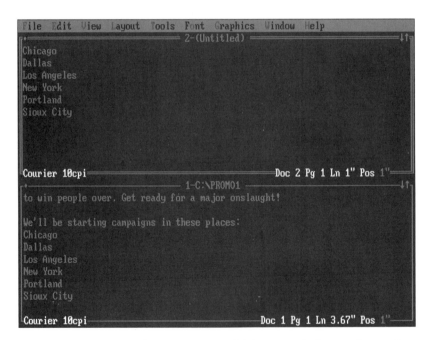

Figure 3-7 You can keep your material in one window and copy it into a second.

"I Can't Remember All These Keystrokes." Getting Help

Key combinations like Alt+F4 for blocking text are a fast way to work because you don't have to take the time to work through menus. But who can remember all those key combinations? You can find the keystrokes for WordPerfect commands (and get other useful information) by remembering just one keystroke—F1, the Help key. You can press it at any time to get Help:

1. Press F1 to see the main Help screen (see Figure 3-8).

2. Press the down arrow five times to highlight Template, and press Enter. You see a complete listing of all the key combinations that go with the Function keys across the top of the keyboard (see Figure 3-9).

3. Press Tab twice to *Cancel*, then press Enter to get out of the Help screen.

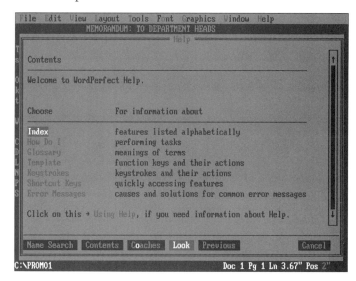

Figure 3-8 You can start here to get help in a number of different forms.

You don't always have to start with the first help screen either.

"I Can't Remember All These Keystrokes." Getting Help (continued)

If you're using a feature, you can press F1 to get help on what you're doing at the time. Try it:

1. This time use keystrokes to open a document. Press Shift+F10 to display the *Open Document* window.

2. To get Help for the open window, press F1. Instead of seeing the Help Contents page, you see Help on opening a document.

3. Press Esc three times to close the Help windows and go back to the document.

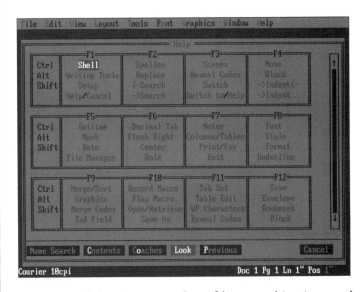

Figure 3-9 Help gives you a list of keys combinations and what they do.

"Whoops. Where Did I Put That?" Search and Replace

If you want to look for a word on a typed page, you have to use your eyes and it may take awhile. WordPerfect, though, will find a word for you as many times as it occurs in your electronic document and give you the option of replacing it with another.

Searching for Something

Suppose you wanted to find each instance of the word *campaign;* here's how to search for a word (or phrase):

1. With PROMO1 still on the screen, press Home, Home, Up arrow to move to the top of the document.

2. Press Alt+e, then h to choose *Search* from the Edit menu. You see a Search window (see Figure 3-10).

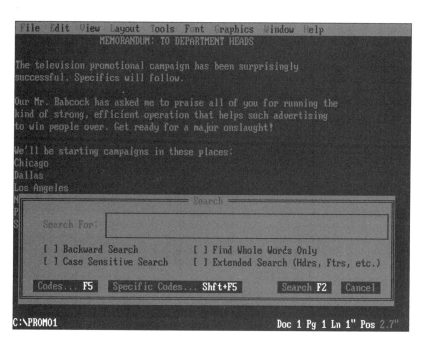

Figure 3-10 Type whatever you want to search for.

3. Type `campaign`.

4. To start the search, press F2. The cursor moves to the word *campaign* in the first line.

5. To find *campaign* again, Press F2 once to open the *Search* window with *campaign* already typed in, and press F2 again to start the search.

Replacing Something When You Find It

You can do more than just find a word. You can substitute another word for it. Suppose that you don't just want to find the word *campaign,* you want to replace it with the word *program.* Again, you start by moving to the beginning of the document:

1. Press Home, Home, Up arrow to move to the top of the document.

2. Choose *Search and Replace* from the Edit menu by pressing Alt+e, then l. WordPerfect displays the *Search and Replace* window (see Figure 3-11).

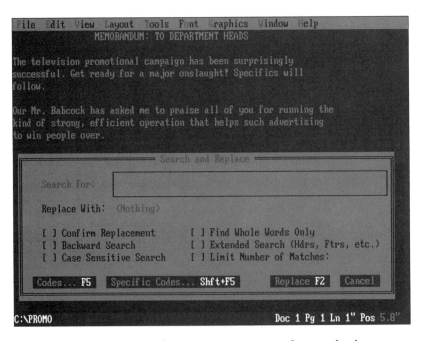

Figure 3-11 State the phrase you want to replace and what you want to put in its place.

3. In the box labeled *Search For,* type `campaign`.

4. Press Tab. A box opens next to *Replace With.*

5. Type `program`, and to start Replace press F2. WordPerfect replaces *campaign* with *program* throughout the document and reports on how many times it did it in a window labeled *Search and Replace Complete.*

6. Press Enter to close the *Search and Replace Complete* window.

Checking Spelling and Finding Synonyms

When you type something on a typewriter, you usually have to check your own spelling. Word processors can do it for you, though, if you just ask. First, go through PROMO1, the document you've been working on, and plant a couple spelling mistakes for WordPerfect to look for:

1. In the second line of the first paragraph, type an extra l so that *successful* becomes *successfull.*

2. In the same line, change *Specifics* to *Specifcs.*

3. Save the document.

Checking Spelling

Now try out the spell checker:

1. Press Home, Home, up arrow to go to the top of the document.

2. Press Alt+t, then w to choose *Writing Tools* from the *Tools* menu.

3. From the submenu, press s for *Spell Check.* The *Spell Check* window opens (Figure 3-12.)

4. Press d to have the spell checker look over the whole document.

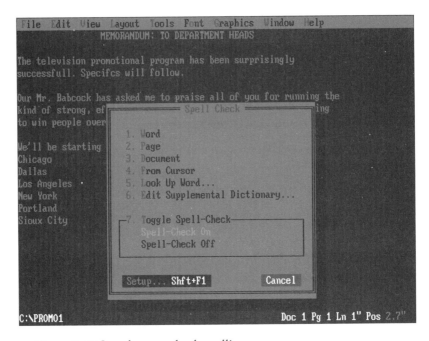

Figure 3-12 Start here to check spelling.

The spell checker shows *successfull* in the *Word Not Found* window and suggests alternatives to it.

6. *Successful* is highlighted and an arrow points to *7. Replace Word*. Press Enter. WordPerfect replaces *successfull* with *successful* and displays *Specifcs* in the *Word Not Found* window. In this case, it doesn't suggest an alternative.

7. Press 4 for *4. Edit Word*.

8. Change *Specifcs* to *Specifics* in the document, then press F7 to exit. When it finds no more mistakes, WordPerfect shows the message *Spell Check Completed*.

9. Press Enter to finish the spell check.

In the typewriter age, misspelled words, repeated words (like "the the"), and typographical errors were just part of the human condition; word processors take a giant step toward eliminating them.

Finding Synonyms

Spell checking can be challenge enough if you have to do it by hand, but at least you have a good chance of having a dictionary handy to help you. Thesauruses for finding synonyms, though, have a way of making themselves scarce. You can't lose the one in WordPerfect; it's built in:

1. Put the cursor anywhere in the word *praise* in the first line of the second paragraph.

2. Press Alt+t to open the *Tools* menu, w to open the *Writing Tools* submenu, and t to start the *Thesaurus*. The *Thesaurus* window lists a number of synonyms for *praise* (see Figure 3-13).

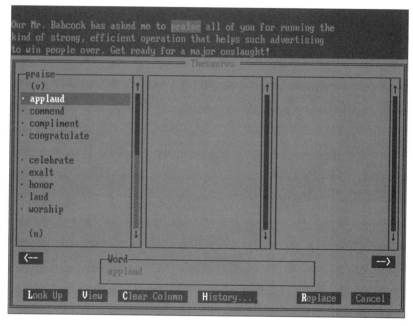

Figure 3-13 WordPerfect's Thesaurus comes built in.

3. Press the down arrow once to highlight commend, then press r for Replace. WordPerfect replaces praise with the synonym from the Thesaurus.

Is there anybody who hasn't done it? The manager says, "This should be about 500 words long," and you end up pointing a finger at the screen and going "one, two, three ." WordPerfect checker will count the words for you, faster than your finger can do it:

Press Alt+t, then w to display the *Writing Tools* submenu, then press d for *Document Info*. A *Document Information* window (Figure 3-14) tells you the word count and a good bit more.

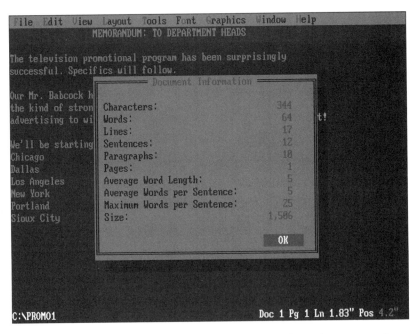

Figure 3-14 The Document Information window shows you the word count and a number of other counts.

"You Mean It'll Spot A Missing Comma?"

You might be able to have a Thesaurus on your desktop, but until now the only place to carry a grammar checker was inside your head. WordPerfect puts one inside the computer. First, put a common grammar mistake into the current document:

> Change the sentence that reads *The television promotional program has been surprisingly successful* to be *The television promotional program have been surprisingly successful.* (In the second sentence, the verb is wrong.)

Now, grammar check the document:

1. Press Alt+t, then w, then g for *Grammatik.* A copyright screen for Grammatik 5 goes by, then a menu screen comes up.

2. To start the check, use the menu at the bottom of the screen. Press i for *Interactive check.* Grammatik suggests a change to the word *program.*

3. Using the menu at the bottom of the screen, press F10 for *Next problem.* Grammatik highlights the sentence you changed just before starting the grammar checker and says *The singular subject program takes a singular verb, not the plural verb have.* (SeeFigure 3-15.)

4. Again using the menu at the bottom of the screen, Press F9 for *Edit problem.* Put the cursor just past the *e* in *have,* press backspace twice to delete *ve,* and type s to restore the verb *has.*

5. To continue the grammar check press F9 for *Recheck from cursor.*

6. Press F10 for *Next problem* as many times as you need until the message comes up saying *Checking complete. Save changes to this document?*

7. To save the changes, press Enter. You go back to the Grammatik 5 opening screen.

8. Use the menu at the bottom to close the grammar checker. Press q for *Quit Grammatik.* You return to your document, where Grammatik puts in the revision you've requested in the grammar checker.

9. Exit from the document and from WordPerfect.

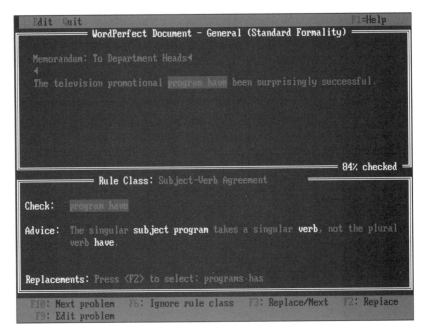

Figure 3.15 The grammar checker finds misused verbs and much more.

By now your typewriter should be just a faint memory. Cut-and-paste, search-and-replace, spell check, finding synonyms, grammar—all of what you can do in WordPerfect, without ever having to worry about misplacing your scissors or your Thesaurus, or changing the ribbon in that noisy old thumper that used to be our best writing tool.

PART II

GETTING DRESSED UP TO GO OUT

When it comes to written work, appearance is very important. In Part II you find out just how powerful WordPerfect is when it comes to appearances. First, you see how to make text bold and italic and how to use a different typeface if you wish. Then you see how to beautify the page by changing the spacing, the margins, and the indenting. Finally, you go beyond text altogether and work with tables, lines, and pictures.

CHAPTER
4

GETTING REALLY BOLD . . .
AND ITALIC, AND MORE

Dressing up a document used to be a job for the local print shop; you'd come up with a draft at home with a pen, and the ink-stained person in the shop would make it all look beautiful. In the age of WordPerfect you still might want to go to the printer for wedding announcements, but, except for the really elaborate jobs, there isn't much that the shop can do that you can't do for yourself. You can create your own dark text, large headlines, fancy typefaces, and more.

As you begin to create a variety of documents, you have to get adept at keeping track of them. In this chapter you also see how to do your electronic filing with WordPerfect.

Getting Bold with Your Text

On many occasions you could dress up a document and make it easier to read just by putting the title and main subheadings into darker type (called *bold* type) than the rest of the text. You'll try that in a minute, but first start WordPerfect and type in a sample document to work with, shown in Figure 4-1:

Type this text, pressing Enter at the end of each paragraph and Enter again to create an extra space between lines:

```
Summer Fun Fest

    Eats . . .Softball. . . Hardball . . . Illegal
Gambling . . . Dancing

    Bring the kids and all your aunts and uncles to our
annual company picnic.

    Here's some details:

    Where: Kataloochi Park, three miles North on
Highway 10

    When: Thursday, July 22 at 3:30 in the afternoon

    Cost: Free (your annual dues covered it all.)

    So be there!
```

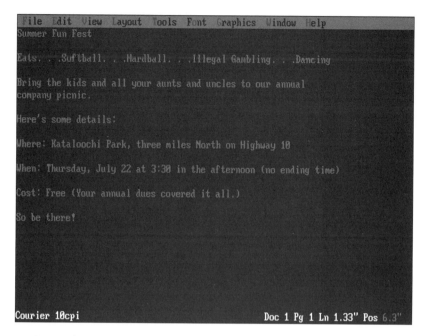

File   Edit   View   Layout   Tools   Font   Graphics   Window   Help
Summer Fun Fest

Eats. . .Softball. . .Hardball. . .Illegal Gambling. . .Dancing

Bring the kids and all your aunts and uncles to our annual
company picnic.

Here's some details:

Where: Kataloochi Park, three miles North on Highway 10

When: Thursday, July 22 at 3:30 in the afternoon (no ending time)

Cost: Free (Your annual dues covered it all.)

So be there!

Courier 10cpi   Doc 1 Pg 1 Ln 1.33" Pos 6.3"

Figure 4-1 A boring-looking sample document, before you get bold
with it.

2. Save the document with the name *Fun*.

If you handed out a flyer that looked like the one in Figure 4-1,
it wouldn't create much excitement no matter what it said. First,
try bolding the title and some of the headings:

1. Select the title, *Summer Fun Fest.*

2. To display the *Font* menu (see Figure 4-2), press Alt+o.

3. To bold the selected text, press b for *Bold.* The text shows up
   as a different color now on your screen, indicating that you've
   formatted it in some way, but later you may not remember
   what the color stands for. (Graphics Mode, shown in a
   moment, solves that problem.)

4. Follow steps 1–3 to bold a few other items—the second line
   (that begins with *Eats*), and also the words *Where:, When:,*
   and *Cost:.*

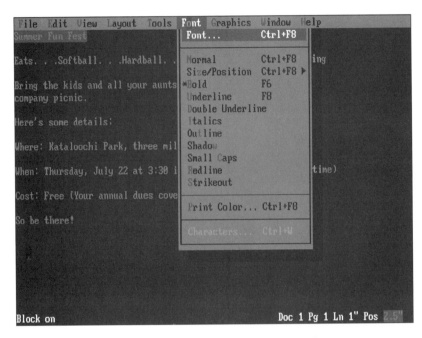

Figure 4-2 Use the Font menu to change the look of your type.

Seeing What You're Going to Get—Graphics Mode

When you're paying attention to the appearance of the words (not just their meaning) you may want to see that appearance as you work. Use Graphics Mode:

With the document still displayed, press Alt+v to display the *View* menu, then press g for *Graphics Mode.* When the document appears on the screen, it looks much more like a real picnic flyer, and less like a computer screen. The bolded letters now show up as bold instead of as a different color (see Figure 4-3). As you work using Graphics Mode you can get a much more realistic feel of what you're actually creating.

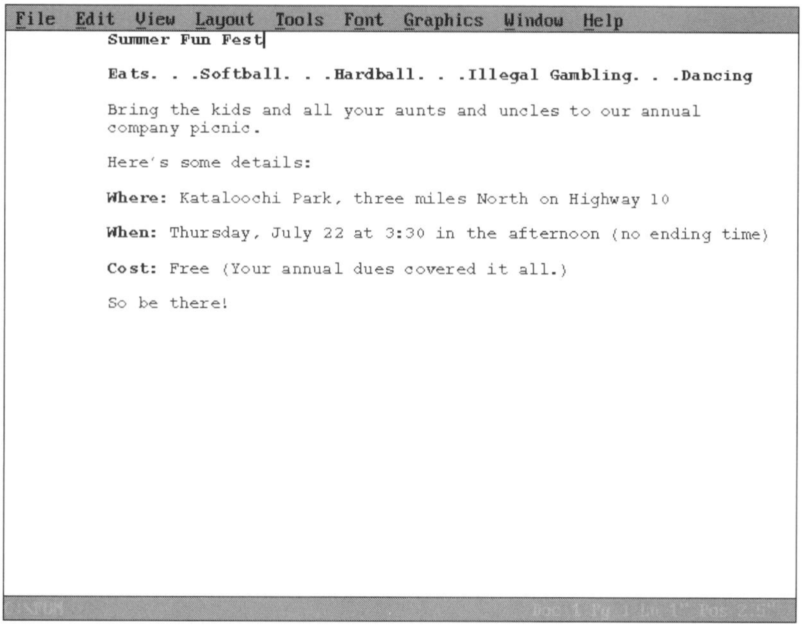

```
File  Edit  View  Layout  Tools  Font  Graphics  Window  Help
     Summer Fun Fest

     Eats. . .Softball. . .Hardball. . .Illegal Gambling. . .Dancing

     Bring the kids and all your aunts and uncles to our annual
     company picnic.

     Here's some details:

     Where: Kataloochi Park, three miles North on Highway 10

     When: Thursday, July 22 at 3:30 in the afternoon (no ending time)

     Cost: Free (Your annual dues covered it all.)

     So be there!
```

Figure 4-3 Graphics Mode shows the page as it will look when you print it.

Adding Italics

Instead of selecting text you've already typed and then changing the font as you did with bolding, you can have text appear in a special font as you type:

1. Put the cursor where you're going to type some new text, just before the *d* in *details* in the line *Here's some details:*.

2. To turn on italics, press the shortcut keys Ctrl+i. (The Ctrl key is in the bottom left or right of the keyboard.)

3. Type `solid` and press the spacebar once. All the new text you type after you press Ctrl+i is in italics.

Changing the Font

WordPerfect starts out using an initial typeface, such as Courier 10cpi. You won't do it now, but you can also change the font itself to one with another name, the same way you've been changing the fonts to bold or italic. To do it, you'd select text, press Alt+o to display the *Font* menu, press o for *Font,* and press f for *Font.* You'd then move the highlight to the new font you wanted to use, press Enter to select it, and choose *OK* to close the window.

Creating Large Headings—Fonts and Sizes

The flyer still is a bit drab, even with some letters in bold and italic. Try changing the size of some text and adding a shadow in one place:

1. Select the first line (*Summer Fun Fest*), then display the Font menu.

2. To display the *Size/Position* submenu, press z (see Figure 4-4).

3. Press e for *Extra Large.* The menus go away, and the title now appears in much larger type than before.

Change the second line to very large type:

1. Select the second line, then display the Font menu and the Size/Position submenu.

2. Press v for *Very Large.*

Make another change to the same line; and a shadow:

Select the second line and display the F<u>o</u>nt menu. Press w for *Shado<u>w</u>.*

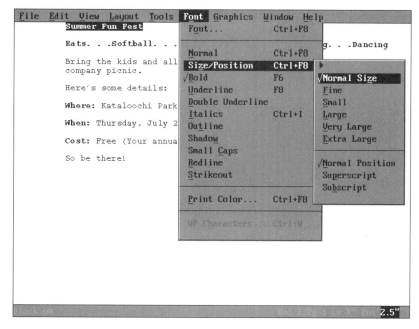

Figure 4-4 Use the Size/Position submenu to change the size of your fonts.

"Where Is That Code to Change the Font?"

As you change fonts and sizes, center text, or make most other changes in your document, you put in hidden codes that tell WordPerfect what to do with the text when it displays it on the screen or prints it on paper. When you've put in quite a few codes, though, you may want to know where they are so that you don't unintentionally, for example, put some text into bold that you want in normal text. Here's how to see the codes in the document::

1. Display the View menu and press c for *Reveal Codes*. A window at the bottom of the screen now shows the text in the document along with all the codes for formatting the text (see Figure 4-5).

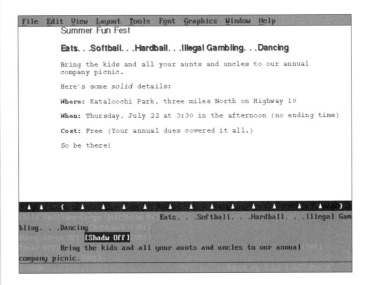

Figure 4-5 Reveal Codes allows you to see the hidden codes in your document.

When you can see the codes, you can readily remove formatting without having to select text and use the menus:1. To take out the code for Very Large On, move the cursor in the document to the start of the second line, just before the word *Eats*. The cursor in the Reveal Codes window goes to the same location.

2. Press Backspace. You delete the code for Very Large On in the Reveal Codes window, and the text changes from very large to normal size in the document window.

For now, put back the code you just deleted:

> *"Where Is That Code to Change the Font?"* (continued)
>
> 1. Press Ctrl+F5 to Undo the change you just made. The code goes back into the document.
>
> 2. To close the Reveal Codes window at the bottom, press Alt+v, then c once again.

Seeing the Printed Page Without Using Up Paper

The picnic flyer you've been developing in this chapter looks pretty realistic when you see it in Graphics Mode, but you may want to see something even closer to the final, printed product. You could always print it to see exactly what it will look like when printed, but WordPerfect gives you a shortcut called *Print Preview:*

1. To display the *Print/Fax* window, press the shortcut keys Shift+F7.

2. To choose *Print Preview,* press 7. The flyer now takes on the exact form it will have when you print it; you can judge the spacing, the fonts, and everything else about the appearance of the page.

3. For a close-up of the page, press Alt+v to display the Print Preview *View menu,* then press i for *Zoom In.*

4. To get a real close-up of the text, repeat step three a couple more times (see Figure 4-6).

You can get a very good idea of what your flyer looks like without having to waste the time and paper to print it.

Now close Print Preview:

1. Press F7. You leave the *Print Preview* window and go back to the document.

Go all the way back to a blank screen:

2. Exit from Fun, so that you have a blank WordPerfect screen.

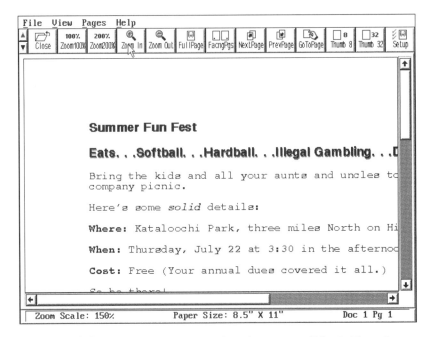

Figure 4-6 Print Preview shows what the page will look like when printed.

"What Are Those Neat Boxes Across the Top?"

You can't use Print Preview without noticing the row of labeled boxes across the top like the one labeled *Zoom Out* with a picture of a magnifying glass on it. Known as *buttons,* these boxes make life easier for people who have a mouse. If you were using a mouse, you'd just point to one of the buttons and click instead of choosing the option from the menu.

3. To switch from Graphics Mode back to Text Mode, press the shortcut key Ctrl+F3, then press 2 in the *Screen* window. (Text Mode runs faster than Graphics Mode.)

Filing Your Work without a File Cabinet

As you work with your electronic documents in WordPerfect, you don't always create paper documents as you would with a typewriter. But you create documents inside the computer, and as time goes by you probably create quite a few of them. It becomes just as important to file these electronic documents in an orderly way as it is with paper documents.

Setting Up Directories

When you're using WordPerfect, you're using MS-DOS, which manages your relationship with the computer hardware. Much of the time you don't have to think about DOS, but it helps to know a little about it when you do the filing with your electronic documents.

Creating a Directory In WordPerfect you can use directories, which are actually DOS directories, the way you use folders in a filing cabinet; you put related material into the same directory. So far you haven't named any specific directory for the couple documents you've created, so they've just gone into the top directory on DOS. You could keep them in their own directory, though. Using DOS commands, follow these steps to create a separate directory in which to keep them without exiting from WordPerfect.

1. Display the File menu, and press f for *File Manager*.

2. In the *Specify File Manager List* window, you state which DOS directory's files you want to look at. To choose a different directory than the one currently used, press F5, for *Redo*.

3. In the *File Manager* window (see Figure 4-7), type h for *Change Default Dir*.

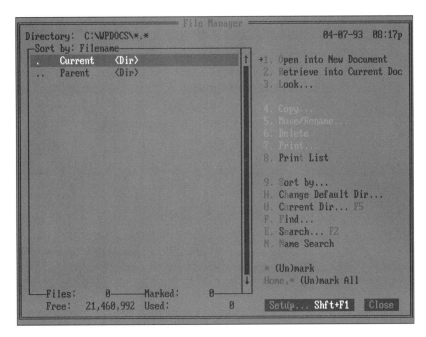

Figure 4-7 Use this window to say where WordPerfect should put your documents most of the time.

4. In the *Change Default Directory* window, type the new directory. It doesn't exist yet, so you'll have the chance to create it. Type C:\WORK. (Be sure to type the *C*, the *:*, and the \, codes that tell DOS where something is.) Press Enter.

5. A window asks. *Create Directory C:\WORK.* Type y for Yes. WordPerfect creates the new directory, which you can think of as a manila folder inside the computer for the documents you make. You return to the File Manager, where you can make the new directory be the one you use all the time.

"I Can't Tell Much from These Names."

When you name a file or a directory in WordPerfect, you again feel the presence of DOS. Because the names have to satisfy DOS requirements, you don't have a lot of freedom.

> *"I Can't Tell Much from These Names." (continued)*
>
> You can't put spaces into the names, so you're limited to one-word names. And the names can be only eight characters long.

Setting Up a Directory as Your Main Directory

Once you've created the new directory you can set it up to be the place where WordPerfect automatically saves your documents:

1. From within the File Manager, press `h` for *Change Default Dir.*

2. This time you'll type a directory that does exist, and it'll become your *default* (primary) directory. Type `C:\WORK` and press Enter.

3. In the *Specify File Manager List* window, press Enter to accept the new directory.

Now WordPerfect will automatically save your new documents into C:\WORK and, in general, will start with that directory whenever you use the File Manager.

When you close your WordPerfect for the day, WordPerfect won't remember to start with that directory. You'll find out later how to set up a permanent default directory. Try out the new default directory:

1. Close the File Manager and return to a blank document screen.

2. Press Alt+f, then `s` to save a document.

3. In the *Save Document 1* window, type the name `new_doc` and press Enter. WordPerfect automatically saves the document into the new default directory you've set up. The name in the bottom left of the screen says `C:\WORK\NEW_DOC`.

Moving a Document

Suppose you wanted to move one of the documents you created before into the new directory:

1. To open the File Manager, press F5.

2. In the *Specify File Manager List* window, press Enter to accept C:\WORK.

3. Now move back up to the directory you were using before you created C:\WORK. In the File Manager window, press the down arrow once to highlight *Parent <Dir>,* and press Enter. You move back up to the top directory, where you filed your first couple of documents for this book.

4. To find the document you want, press n for *Name Search.*

5. In the *Name Search* window that appears at the bottom left, type FUN. WordPerfect highlights the name of the file you created earlier in this chapter. Press Enter. You've selected a file to move, and you're ready to move it:

1. Press 5 for *Move/Rename.* A *Move/Rename* window comes up, with the file's name in it (see Figure 4-8).

2. Type C:\WORK\FUN and press Enter. WordPerfect moves the file to the new directory.

3. Close the File Manager and return to the document.

Copying a Document

To copy a paper document, you need a copy machine. If the document has several pages, you may have to take awhile, and you may end up putting the pages back in order by hand when you're done. With WordPerfect you can make electronic copies without hassles:

1. Press F5 to open the File Manager and press Enter to accept the default directory in the Specify File Manager List window.

2. In the File Manager, highlight *FUN*, the document you created earlier in the chapter.

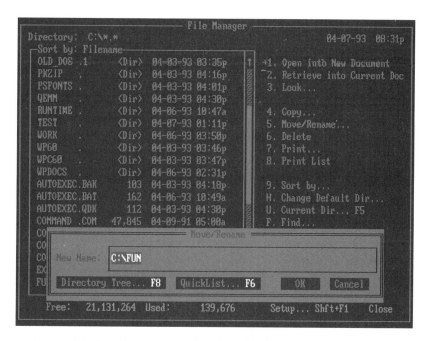

Figure 4-8 Type the new location for a file here.

3. Press 4 for *Copy.*

4. In the *Copy* window (see Figure 4-9), press the End key to go to the end of the line, and type 2, so that the name is now *C:\WORK\FUN2.*

5. Press Enter. You go back to the File Manager, where you now see both *FUN* and *FUN2.* Stay right in the File Manager, which you can also use to delete files.

Deleting a Document

Maybe your computer can hold more stuff than you ever imagined, but it can still run out of space eventually. Besides, there's no point in keeping files that you never use; they just clutter up your directories and make it harder to find the files you do want. Suppose you wanted to delete the extra copy you just made:

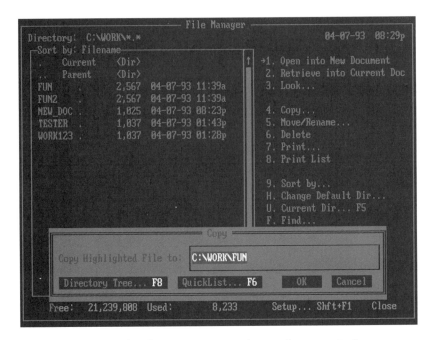

Figure 4-9 To make electronic copies, change the name in here.

1. In the File Manager (still open from the previous steps), highlight *FUN2*.

2. Press d. A message comes up asking if you want to delete the file (see Figure 4-10). Think carefully and, when in doubt, don't delete.

3. Press y for Yes. WordPerfect deletes the file; as you can see, it's no longer listed in the File Manager window.

4. Close the File Manager.

5. Close the open document and exit from WordPerfect.

Your WordPerfect documents can come to life as you introduce large type, bold or italic type, and much more. In WordPerfect 6.0, too, you can choose to see the fonts right on the WordPerfect screen as you work.

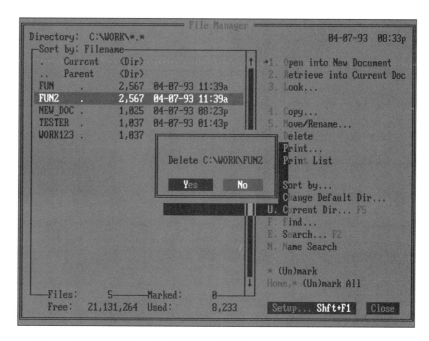

Figure 4-10 Think twice before deleting.

"I'd Like a Few Carbon Copies"

Besides making electronic copies of documents, there is a way to make multiple copies of what you print, something you'll find much easier than working with carbon copies on a typewriter:

Use the shortcut keys Shift+F7 to display the *Print* Window (see Figure 4-11).

There's no reason to do it now, but if you wanted to print more than one copy of your document, you'd press n to put the cursor in the line that says *Number of Copies* and then type in the number of copies you wanted.

"I'd Like a Few Carbon Copies" (continued)

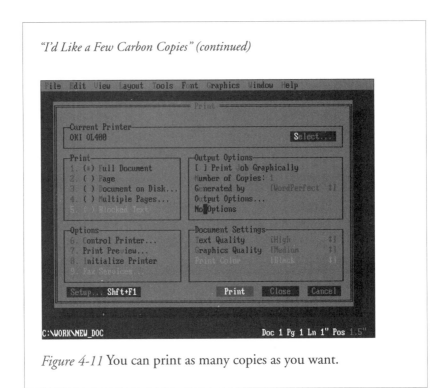

Figure 4-11 You can print as many copies as you want.

As you create more and more documents, of course, you're going to have to file them so that you can readily keep track of them. Now you know how to do that.

In the next chapter you see another way to make your documents look the way you want, by working with the spacing and other elements of the page layout.

CHAPTER

5

ORDERING YOUR PAGE AROUND

Once you get used to it, working with pages is just as easy on a word processor as on a typewriter; but it might not seem that way at first. After all, on a typewriter the physical pages are there in front of you. To type in the top margin on a typewriter, you just roll the page up so you're in the margin. To set a side margin, you can look at the page as you set it. On a word processor you do have to find out how to get into the top margin or set a left margin. Once you know how, though, automation takes over, and the word processor once again is at least as easy as the typewriter and more powerful than all but the most advanced electronic typewriters.

Working with More than One Page

If you don't do anything, your pages still come out looking good in WordPerfect, because WordPerfect automatically puts in margins and page breaks for you. Try typing a document with more than one page, and see what happens. Type in this sample document and watch what happens when you finish a page. (If you don't feel like doing that much typing, type part of the document, then just hold down Enter until WordPerfect automatically starts a new page):

```
Monthly Report

Sales Last Month

This has been a difficult month for the sales force,
but we have every reason to be optimistic about next
month. It's true that sales of our main product were
down almost 25% from what they were last year. But
those figures are misleading, because we've lowered
prices so much that our increased sales don't show up
as increased revenues.

Increased Leads

But our number of sales leads actually increased by
50%. We see that as a strong sign of better marketing
and advertising.

Also, we're developing new sales districts that we
believe are very, very promising for future sales. Our
```

competition has been working in those districts with Moderate success. We've outsold them most other places and expect to do the same there as well.

These are the regions we're looking at closely:

Upper mountain area

Suburban Centerville

Outer River Area

Automated Reporting

We're adding an automated reporting system that should help us book sales faster than before, and that should show up at the front end before long, too. Faster bookings do create more free time for the sales people, which they can then invest in canvassing for additional sales.

Better Training Sessions

We're bringing in Tom Frederick, the top salesman for the Northwest district and now a Regional Manager, and he's heading up a group of training sessions for us this month. Our people will pick up on his enthusiasm as well as his selling techniques, and we believe his training will impact the bottom line just about right away.

Promotions and Salary Increases

Everybody always likes to experience success, and nothing rewards a successful person better than more money and power. We've recommended several promotions and salary increases to upper management. If these go through, we believe they'll result in still stronger sales performance from our top people.

Recommendations for Advertising

We're finding that the "Fly Us" campaign isn't getting quite the results we had hoped for. Some people are confused and think we're an airline company. We'd like

```
to make some additional recommendations and will do so
in the next meeting.

List of Trade Shows We Should Attend

On a separate page we're listing the trade shows we
think we should definitely attend, even if we do plan
to cut back on some of our trade show presentations
next year.
```

You don't have to do anything to get automatic page breaks, and, unlike with a typewriter, you don't have to worry about accidentally going too far on the page and having to retype the whole thing.

Putting in Your Own Page Breaks

Sometimes you want to have the page always break at a certain point, such as at the end of a chapter or just before a list. Here's how to put in your own page break, but only use it when you need it. Otherwise you'll lose the benefit of having WordPerfect automatically make your pages the same size:

1. To put the cursor at the end of the document, press Home, Home, Down arrow.

2. To put in the permanent page break (see Figure 5-1), press Ctrl+Enter. WordPerfect puts in the break. The line for the break shows up only on the screen, not on your printed page.

"How Do I Type in the Top Margin?" Adding Numbers

Typewriters may seem better at first for adding page numbers; you just roll the page to where you want it and type. Once you find out how to type in the margin with WordPerfect, though, you get many advantages over a word processor: You only type a number once, and numbers appear on all the pages. The numbers always appear in the same place on the page and with the same format. If you add an extra page, WordPerfect renumbers automatically. Here's what to do:

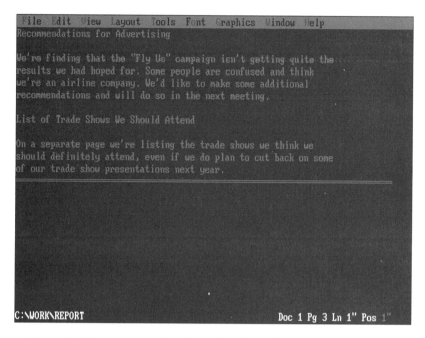

Figure 5-1 You can see a hard page break on the screen.

1. Put the cursor anywhere on the first page of the document, and from the Layout menu, choose *Page.*

2. To tell WordPerfect to use numbering, in the *Page Format window,* type n for *Page Numbering.*

3. To say where you want the number on the page, in the *Page Numbering window* (see Figure 5-2), press p for *Page Number Position.*

4. In the *Page Number Position* window, press e for *Top Center,* and choose *OK.* To return to the document, also choose *OK* In the Page Numbering and Page Format windows.

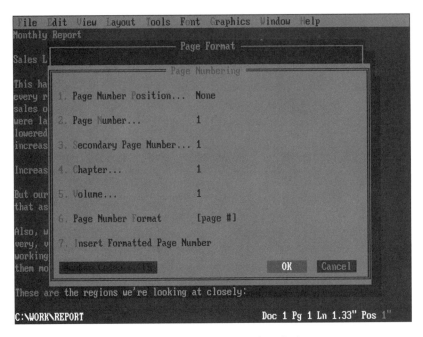

Figure 5-2 Here set up the page numbers for all the pages.

"How Do I Know My Number's There?"

Once you've created your header, you still can't see it to be sure it's there. To see it, try this:

Display the View menu and press a for *Page Mode.*

You can see the page the way it really appears, with headers, footers, margins, indents, spacing, and so on. The number for the page shows clearly at the top where you put it (see Figure 5-3).

"How Do I Know My Number's There?" (cont.)

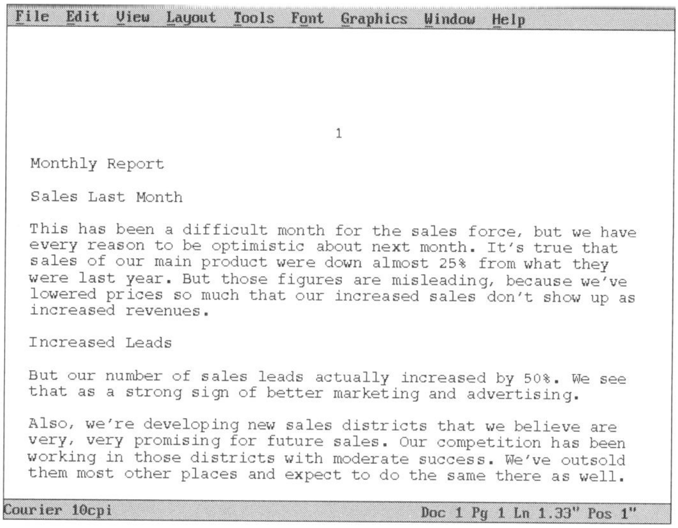

```
File  Edit  View  Layout  Tools  Font  Graphics  Window  Help




                                  1

      Monthly Report

      Sales Last Month

      This has been a difficult month for the sales force, but we have
      every reason to be optimistic about next month. It's true that
      sales of our main product were down almost 25% from what they
      were last year. But those figures are misleading, because we've
      lowered prices so much that our increased sales don't show up as
      increased revenues.

      Increased Leads

      But our number of sales leads actually increased by 50%. We see
      that as a strong sign of better marketing and advertising.

      Also, we're developing new sales districts that we believe are
      very, very promising for future sales. Our competition has been
      working in those districts with moderate success. We've outsold
      them most other places and expect to do the same there as well.

Courier 10cpi                                Doc 1 Pg 1 Ln 1.33" Pos 1"
```

Figure 5-3 In Page Mode you can see your number at the top and much more.

Being Sensitive to Widows and Orphans

Many people don't like to have a last line of a paragraph appearing alone at the top of a page (a *widow*) or the first line appearing alone at the bottom (an *orphan*). You can prevent them automatically:

1. Go to the top of the document, display the Layout menu, then press o for *Other.*

2. In the *Other Format* window, (see Figure 5-4), press w for *Widow/Orphan Protect,* then choose *OK.* WordPerfect will take care of widows and orphans from the point where you put the code in the document to do so.

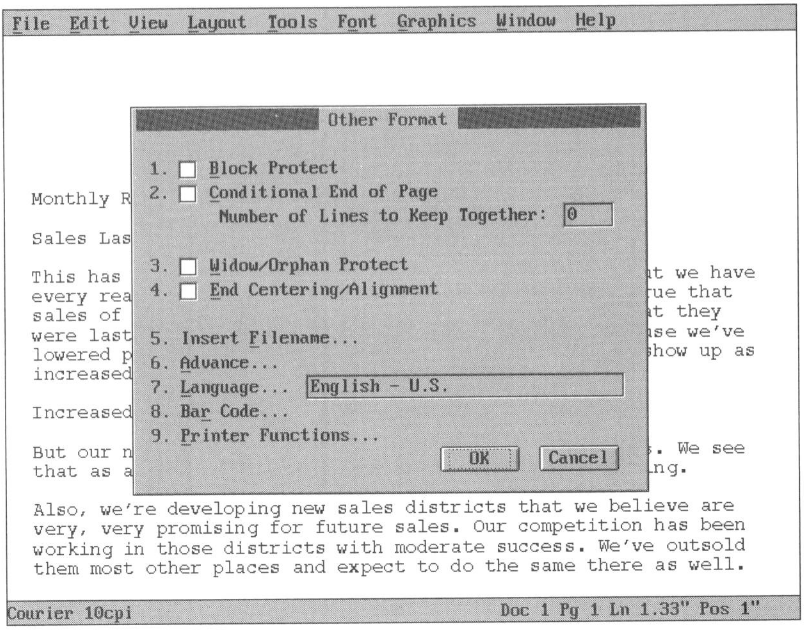

```
┌──────────────────────────────────────────────────────────┐
│  File  Edit  View  Layout  Tools  Font  Graphics  Window  Help │
├──────────────────────────────────────────────────────────┤
│                                                            │
│          ┌────────────── Other Format ──────────────┐      │
│          │                                           │      │
│          │  1. ☐ Block Protect                       │      │
│  Monthly R│  2. ☐ Conditional End of Page            │      │
│          │      Number of Lines to Keep Together: ☐ 0│      │
│  Sales Las│                                           │      │
│          │  3. ☐ Widow/Orphan Protect                │t we have│
│  This has │  4. ☐ End Centering/Alignment             │ue that  │
│  every rea│                                           │t they   │
│  sales of │  5. Insert Filename...                    │se we've │
│  were last│  6. Advance...                            │how up as│
│  lowered p│  7. Language...  English - U.S.           │         │
│  increased│  8. Bar Code...                           │         │
│  Increased│  9. Printer Functions...                  │         │
│          │                   ┌────────┐ ┌────────┐   │         │
│  But our n│                   │   OK   │ │ Cancel │   │. We see │
│  that as a│                   └────────┘ └────────┘   │ng.      │
│          └───────────────────────────────────────────┘      │
│  Also, we're developing new sales districts that we believe are│
│  very, very promising for future sales. Our competition has been│
│  working in those districts with moderate success. We've outsold│
│  them most other places and expect to do the same there as well.│
├──────────────────────────────────────────────────────────┤
│ Courier 10cpi                         Doc 1 Pg 1 Ln 1.33" Pos 1" │
└──────────────────────────────────────────────────────────┘
```

Figure 5-4 Here take care of widows and orphans.

Moving among Your Pages

Finding a page among typed pages is pretty easy; just flip to the page with your fingers. In WordPerfect it might not seem so easy at first. The pages are one, long document. There's a way, though:

1. From the Edit menu, choose *Go To.*

2. In the *Go To* window, type 2 to go to page 2.

Using Double Spacing

Once you've typed a page on a typewriter, you don't want someone to ask you to double space it; that means typing it all over again. With WordPerfect, though, you can double space with a single command (and, by the way, the pages renumber themselves automatically.) Try it:

1. Go to the top of the document, display the Layout menu, then, to display the window where you change line spacing, press 1 for *Line*.

2. Press Tab several times to move to the *Line Spacing*, type 2, press Enter, and choose *OK*. All the lines beginning from where you have the cursor are now double spaced (see Figure 5-5).

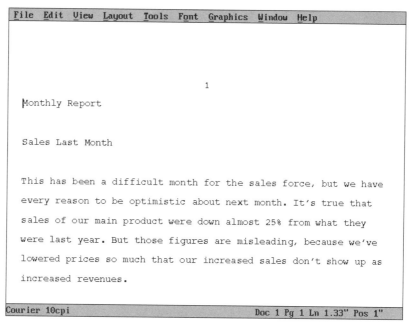

```
File  Edit  View  Layout  Tools  Font  Graphics  Window  Help




                            1

Monthly Report


Sales Last Month


This has been a difficult month for the sales force, but we have

every reason to be optimistic about next month. It's true that

sales of our main product were down almost 25% from what they

were last year. But those figures are misleading, because we've

lowered prices so much that our increased sales don't show up as

increased revenues.

Courier 10cpi                              Doc 1 Pg 1 Ln 1.33" Pos 1"
```

Figure 5-5 One code double spaces every line following the code.

Changing the Shape of the Page—Margins

Setting margins in WordPerfect is mechanical, and you can be precise about the sizes of the margin and the size of the page. Next you'll see how to set the margins just as precisely as on any typewriter:

1. From the Layout menu, press m for *Margins*.

Before you change them, all the margins are 1 inch (see Figure 5-6).

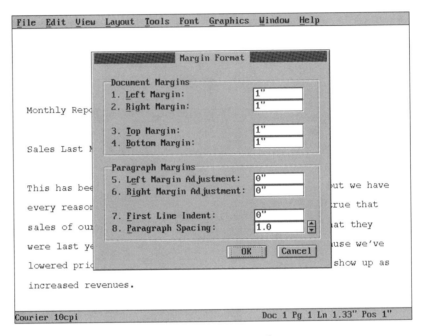

Figure 5-6 At first, all the margins are 1 inch.

2. Press Tab until the cursor is in the box next to *Left Margin,* then type 1.5" and press Enter. Press Enter to close the *Margin Format* window and go back to the document. The wider margin shows up on the page.

"How Can You Justify That?"

Justification, a printing term, means having the line come exactly flush to the margin. Most text you see is left justified. You can have both ends of the line, left and right, be flush against their respective margins.

"How Can You Justify That?" (continued)

1. Select the first full paragraph in the document, beginning *This has been.*2. Display the Layout menu, then press j for *Justification* and f for *Full*. Each end of the line goes all the way to the margin (see Figure 5-7).

3. Repeat steps 1 to 3, then choose *Left* to go back to the justification you had before.

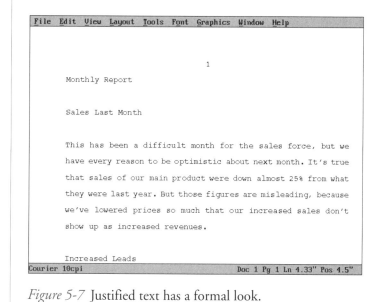

Figure 5-7 Justified text has a formal look.

Picking Up the Tabs

You can always change the margins for certain paragraphs to indent just those paragraphs, but working with margins is cumbersome for indenting paragraphs; use tabs instead.

Indenting with the Tab Key

WordPerfect comes with tabs already set at 1.5". To indent a line that much, just press the Tab key the same way you would on a typewriter:

1. Put the cursor at the start of the first full paragraph, and press Tab once. You indent the first line in the familiar way (see Figure 5-8).

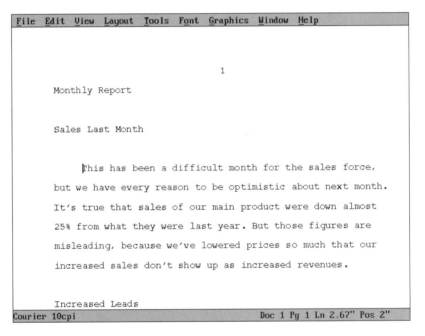

Figure 5-8 Press tab to indent the preset amount.

2. Press Backspace to delete the tab and move the line back flush with the margin.

"But I Want to Set My Own Tabs!"

You can decide for yourself to have as many tabs as you want and in whatever positions you want. Here's how to set tabs:

1. Display the Layout menu, and press t for _Tab Set._ The window shows where the tabs are now; each small arrow in the ruler stands for a left tab (a tab that appears to the left of the material it indents). See Figure 5-9. You won't do it now, but if you wanted to change the settings you'd choose the type of tab you wanted, and you'd set the distance between tabs with the _Set Tab_ box.

2. Press Cancel to close the Tab Set window without changing any tabs.

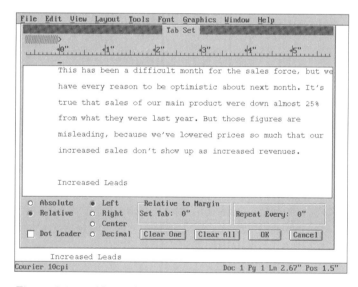

Figure 5-9 You'd use this window to position your own tabs.

Indenting a Complete Paragraph

An old-fashioned way to indent is to press Tab at the start of each line you want to indent. You can do a whole lot more than just press Tab to indent lines. Suppose you wanted to indent a whole paragraph:

1. Put the cursor at the end of the words *Monthly Report* at the top and press Enter twice to put the cursor by itself at the start of a blank line.

2. From the Layout menu, press a for *Alignment* then i for *Indent.* All the lines you type will be indented from the left.

3. To see actual indented text, type this quotation: `"The key to any successful sales effort, we've found again and again, is being aggressive and friendly at the same time."` Note that WordPerfect automatically indents each line, not just the first.

"I Like to Indent Quotes from Both Sides."

Often when you indent a paragraph you want to indent it equally from both sides, but if you're doing that by hand you have to remember to press Tab at the correct times. It can get tricky. WordPerfect has a setting for it, though:

1. First, prepare the paragraph for the new code. Put the cursor at the start of the paragraph you just indented, and press Backspace to delete the hidden indent code. You're ready to put in a new tab.

2. From the Layout menu, choose *Alignment,* then press n for *Indent -><-.* WordPerfect indents both sides of the line (see Figure 5-10).

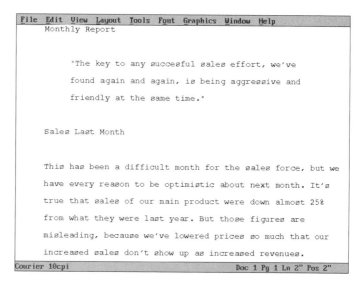

"I Like to Indent Quotes from Both Sides." (continued)

```
File  Edit  View  Layout  Tools  Font  Graphics  Window  Help
      Monthly Report


          "The key to any succesful sales effort, we've
          found again and again, is being aggressive and
          friendly at the same time."


      Sales Last Month


      This has been a difficult month for the sales force, but we
      have every reason to be optimistic about next month. It's
      true that sales of our main product were down almost 25%
      from what they were last year. But those figures are
      misleading, because we've lowered prices so much that our
      increased sales don't show up as increased revenues.
Courier 10cpi                              Doc 1 Pg 1 Ln 2" Pos 2"
```

Figure 5-10 With one code you can indent both sides of a paragraph.

Indenting Just the First Line

With a single code you can indent all the rest of the lines in a paragraph after the first, something known as a *hanging indent.* Try it:

1. Put the cursor at the beginning of the first full paragraph, which begins *This has been,* then from the Layout menu press a for *Alignment.*

2. For *Hanging Indent,* press h. WordPerfect indents all lines after the first, a layout you may find attractive for overheads, reports and other brief presentations (see Figure 5-11).

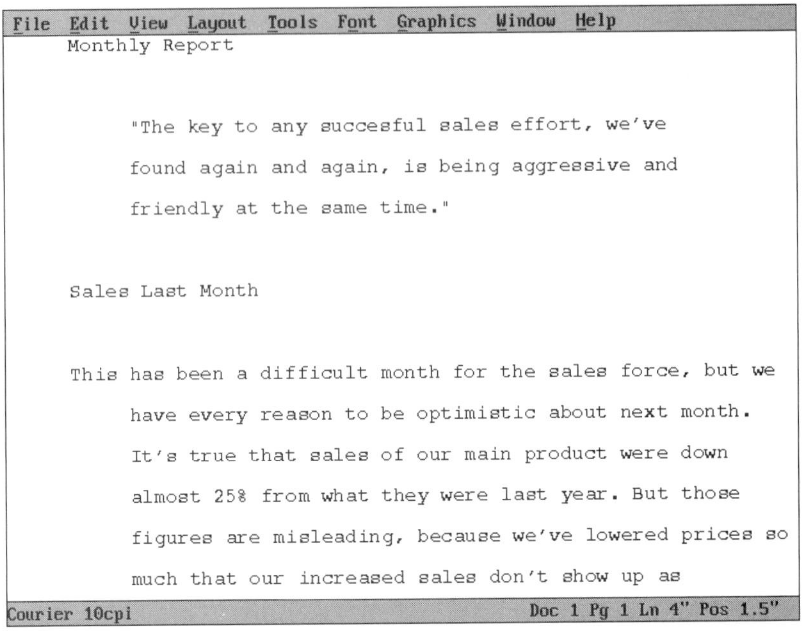

```
 File  Edit  View  Layout  Tools  Font  Graphics  Window  Help
        Monthly Report


           "The key to any succesful sales effort, we've

           found again and again, is being aggressive and

           friendly at the same time."


        Sales Last Month


        This has been a difficult month for the sales force, but we

            have every reason to be optimistic about next month.

            It's true that sales of our main product were down

            almost 25% from what they were last year. But those

            figures are misleading, because we've lowered prices so

            much that our increased sales don't show up as
 Courier 10cpi                                    Doc 1 Pg 1 Ln 4" Pos 1.5"
```

Figure 5-11 A hanging indent calls attention to the start of a paragraph.

3. Go back to Text Mode.

4. Save the document with the name MONTH, so you can use it again briefly in a later chapter.

5. Exit from the document and from WordPerfect.

When you work with the page on your computer screen, then, you take control just as readily as on a typewriter. Thanks to Page Mode, the screen looks like an actual page with margins and spacing. You can then take care of such old standbys as breaks, page numbers, margins, and tabs by choosing commands from menus.

Even tables of multiple rows and columns are automatic in word processing, as you see in the next chapter.

CHAPTER

6

GOING BEYOND WORDS— TO ROWS, COLUMNS, AND PICTURES

WordPerfect, as its name suggests, specializes in handling words, but it can do things with rows, columns, numbers, lines, boxes, and pictures as well. Anyone who has ever attempted it knows that creating a table can be a typist's nightmare, but a table isn't a WordPerfect user's nightmare. Boxes and pictures are also often tricky in the old medium, but not in this new one. Even a table of contents, rather slow and painstaking if you use the typewriter approach, can be automatic in WordPerfect.

Creating a Table

Sooner or later, usually sooner, almost everyone in an office has to create a table. WordPerfect simplifies it to a process of filling in the blanks.

Suppose you wanted to create a table with this information:

Sales Person	Q1	Q2	Q3	Total to Date
Ron	24000	13000	18000	
Jessica	19000	27000	12000	
Shane	15000	16000	15000	
Allison	11000	10000	25000	

First you create a blank table; then you fill it in.

1. Start WordPerfect, make C:\WORK your default directory; and save a file with the name C:\WORK\sales_tb. Put a centered title at the top saying Sales Results. You're ready to start a table:

2. Put the cursor at the start of a blank line, display the Layout menu, press b for *Tables*, then in the *Tables* submenu (see Figure 6-1), press c for *Create*.

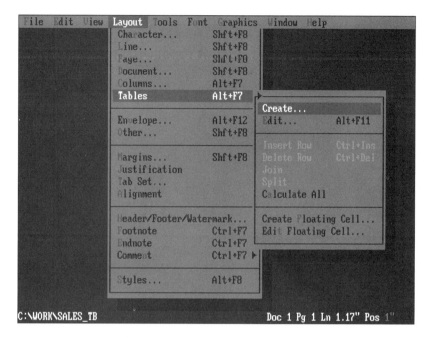

Figure 6-1 Use this submenu for working with tables.

You have to say how many columns and rows you want. (You can change it later, if you want.) Rows go across the page, and columns go down.

3. For *Columns,* type 5, and press Tab.

4. For *Rows,* type 5 again, and press Enter. Choose *OK.*

A table with the right number of rows and columns appears on the screen. You don't type text in this screen; it's for editing the structure of rows, columns, and cells in the table.

5. To exit from Table Edit and go back to the document, press F7. A nice, blank table awaits you (see Figure 6-2).

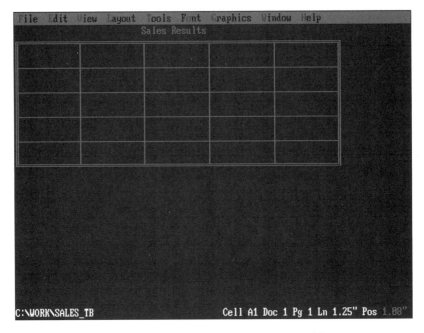

Figure 6-2 Once you set up a blank table, you just fill it in.

Filling in the Table

Once you let WordPerfect set up the rows and columns of your table for you, you don't have to think about the sizes of the squares you fill in or where to place lines or anything else to do with tables. You just type:

1. If the cursor isn't in the top left already, put it there with the arrow keys. Type `Sales Person`, and press Tab.

2. Continue to fill in the table so that it looks like the one in Figure 6-3. Use the Tab key to move forwards, Shift+Tab to move backwards.

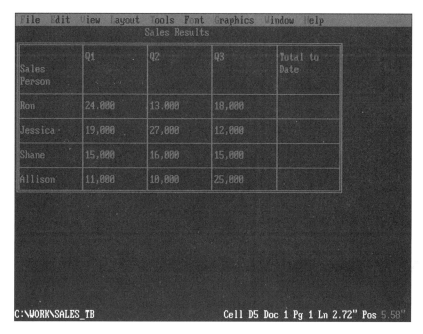

Figure 6-3 The filled-in table.

Once you let WordPerfect set up your rows and columns, making a table is a matter of typing and pressing the tab key—a far cry from the ordeal of trying to line everything up using the tab key on many typewriters.

Changing the Size of Rows and Columns

Once you have your table in place, you'll probably see ways you could make it look better. To change the format of the table itself (rather than the words in the table), you edit it:

1. With the cursor anywhere in the table, display the Layout menu and the Tables submenu, then press e for *Edit*. Now the edit screen shows your filled-in table, but you don't change the words here (see Figure 6-4).

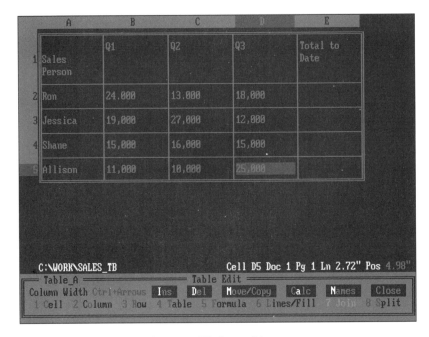

Figure 6-4 You can edit your filled-in table.

2. To change the width of a column, highlight the cell in the top left, and press 2 for *Column.* A Column Format window comes up (see Figure 6-5).

3. To go to *Width,* press w , and type 1.5". Press Enter twice to leave the window.

4. Repeat the steps to make columns two through four 1" wide and column five 1.5" wide. Don't leave the table editor yet; there's more you can do to dress up the table.

Adding Dark Lines

A table looks neat to begin with, but you can make it more attractive in a number of ways. Dark lines can really dress it up:

1. With the Table Edit window still at the bottom of the screen, press 6 for *Lines/Fill.*

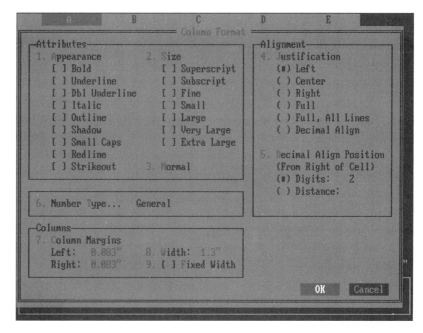

Figure 6-5 Use this window to change the look of a column.

2. To change the lines around the outside of the table, work with the border. In the *Table Lines* window, press e for *Border/Fill.*

3. In the *Table Border/Fill* window, press b for *Border Style.*

4. In the *Border Styles* window, move the highlight to *Extra Thick Border* and press s for *Select.*

5. Close the Table Border/Fill window and the Table Lines window.

6. Press F7 to go back to the document and see the edited table with a border around it.

7. To see a Print Preview of the table, press Shift+F7, then v and zoom in twice (see Figure 6-6).

8. Press F7 to leave Print Preview.

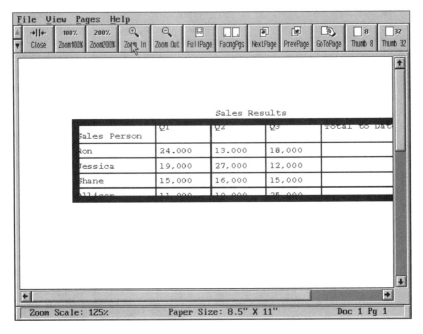

Figure 6-6 You can add a dark border to the table.

The Word Processor as Number Processor?

You don't have to use tables to do math in WordPerfect, but a table is often a handy place to do some simple math. Try it in the sample table:

1. Start where you want to have the result of the math. Put the cursor in column five, row two (the blank cell right under Total to Date).

2. Again choose *Tables* from the Layout menu, then choose Edit.

3. Choose a command from the Table Edit window for math. Type 5 for *Formula,* then, in the *Table Formula* window, press F5 for functions.

4. As in a spreadsheet, when you put the functions in the table, they cause the table to do mathematical operations

The Word Processor as Number Processor? (continued)

wherever you put the functions. Type *sum* to choose the SUM(list) formula, then press Enter.

5. Complete the formula so that WordPerfect will know to add the cells across the row. In the Table Formula window fill in the formula so that it reads *SUM(B2+C2+D2),* and choose *OK.*

WordPerfect adds up the three cells and puts the result in the column labeled *Total to Date.*

To get the result for the other sales people, copy the formula to the other cells in the column:

1. With the cursor in cell E2, press m for *Move/Copy,* p for *Copy,* and d for *Down.*

2. Tell it how many cells to copy the fomula into. In the *How Many?* box, type 3 and choose *OK.* WordPerfect calculates the total sales for the other three sales people (see Figure 6-7).

3. Save the changed document.

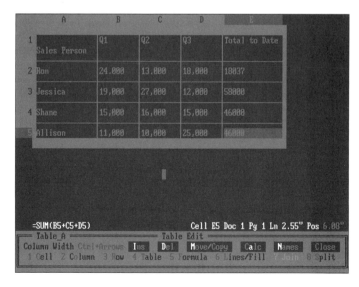

Figure 6-7 WordPerfect calculates everyone's sales results.

"Wait, I Want the List in Alphabetical Order"

Tables are not a requirement for sorting things in WordPerfect any more than they are for doing math, but they're often a handy place to do it. Suppose you wanted to sort the table alphabetically by names:

1. To keep from sorting the top rows (headings) with the others, first choose *Tables* from the Layout menu, then *Edit.*

2. Show which row to change. Put the cursor in the top row and press 3 for *Row.*

3. Change the row to a header row (which won't sort.) In the *Row Format* window (see Figure 6-8), type h for *Header Row* and choose *OK.*

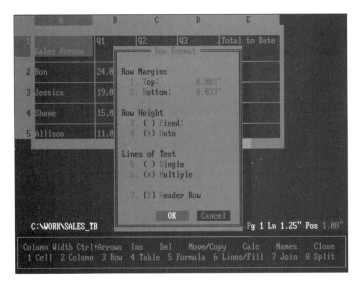

Figure 6-8 When you format a row as a header, it stays in place when you sort the rows.

"Wait, I Want to List in Alphabetical Order" (continued)

4. Press F7 to close the Table Edit window.

Now you're ready to sort:

1. With the cursor anywhere in the table, press Alt+t to open the *Tools* menu and `r` to open the *Sort* window (see Figure 6-9).

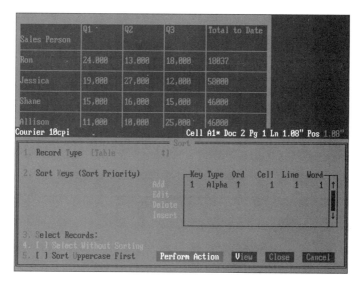

Figure 6-9 Use this window to set up the sort.

In this window, you give WordPerfect instructions for sorting. In this case you don't need to make any changes. WordPerfect is going to sort all the rows, in alphabetical order according to what is in the first cell (see Figure 6-10).

2. Choose Perform Action. WordPerfect sorts the table in alphabetical order. If you wanted, you could sort the sales people another useful way—according to total sales to date—but you won't do that now.

"Wait, I Want to List in Alphabetical Order" (continued)

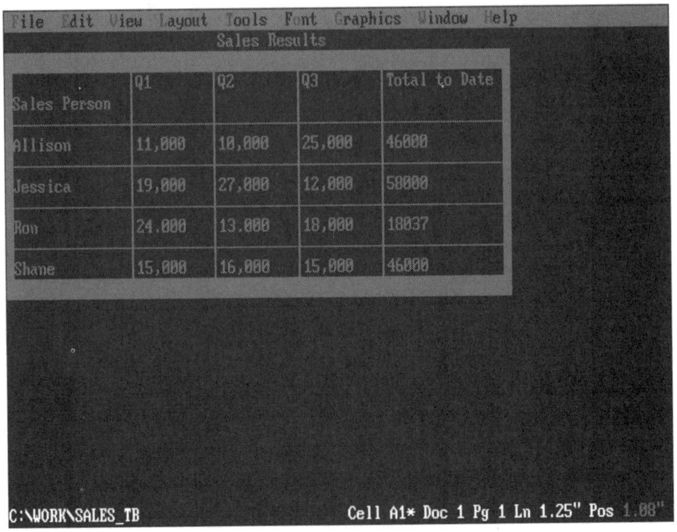

Figure 6-10 WordPerfect sorts alphabetically.

"I Want to Use My Own Spreadsheet!"

You can use spreadsheet functions in a WordPerfect table, just as you might in Lotus 1-2-3, Excel, or another spreadsheet. You may prefer creating your spreadsheets in a real spreadsheet, though. You may bring a spreadsheet into WordPerfect and work with it as either a table or text. You won't actually import a spreadsheet now, but you can see how to do it, then close the window without actually importing one:

From the Tools menu, choose *Spreadsheet,* then, from the submenu, choose *Import.* The *Import Spreadsheet* window opens (see Figure 6-11).

"I Want to Use My Own Spreadsheet!" (continued)

Here you would type in the name of your spreadsheet file, which WordPerfect would then bring in as a table you could work with just as you've worked with the table in this chapter. For now, though, close the *Import Spreadsheet* window without using it.

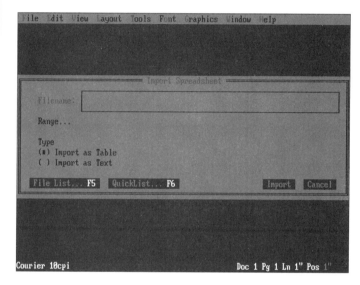

Figure 6-11 From here you can bring a spreadsheet file into WordPerfect.

Putting in Lines and Pictures

Darkening the lines around the table enhanced its look, but you can put in lines and boxes in other ways as well to dress up your documents. You can draw lines using old typewriter methods, but you can also put in an assortment of nice-looking lines that WordPerfect creates for you.

Drawing Lines the Old Typewriter Way

You can draw lines quickly the same way you always drew them on a typewriter:

1. In the same document you've been working on, press Home, Home, End to put the cursor below the Sales Results table.

2. To center the line, press Shift+F6, then hold down the Hyphen key until the line spans the page.

3. In the next section you'll draw a better line, so delete the one you just drew.

Drawing Lines the Word Processing Way

As is so often the case, there are advantages to doing things the WordPerfect way. You can draw lines faster and better:

1. So you can see the results of your changes, press Ctrl+F3, then g to switch to Graphics Mode.

2. Put the cursor at the end of the document, below the table, and press Enter twice to put in additional blank lines.

3. Press Alt+g to open the *Graphics* menu, and 1 for *Graphics Lines.*

4. Press c for *Create.*

5. In the *Create Graphics Line* window (see Figure 6-12), accept all the suggested settings. Choose *OK.* WordPerfect draws a nice, smooth line in your text (see Figure 6-13). You don't have to worry about centering it, going too far when you type it and having to delete it, or any of the other problems you run into when drawing it manually.

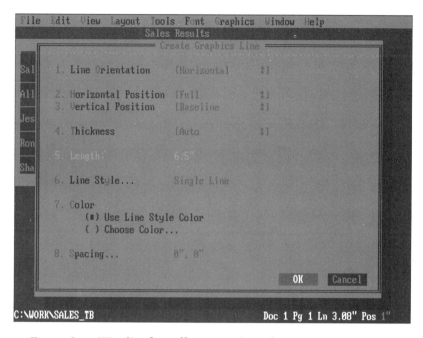

Figure 6-12 WordPerfect offers a number of settings for your lines.

6. Close the file.

To see the line, use the View menu to switch to Graphics Mode. Once you've viewed it, remain in Graphics Mode for the next section.

Drawing Boxes for Graphics and Text

Lines in themselves are attractive, but boxes can be really snazzy. Boxes are great for displaying pictures, for instance. (You can draw boxes using your word processor like a typewriter, but they're so much trouble that almost no one ever does it.)

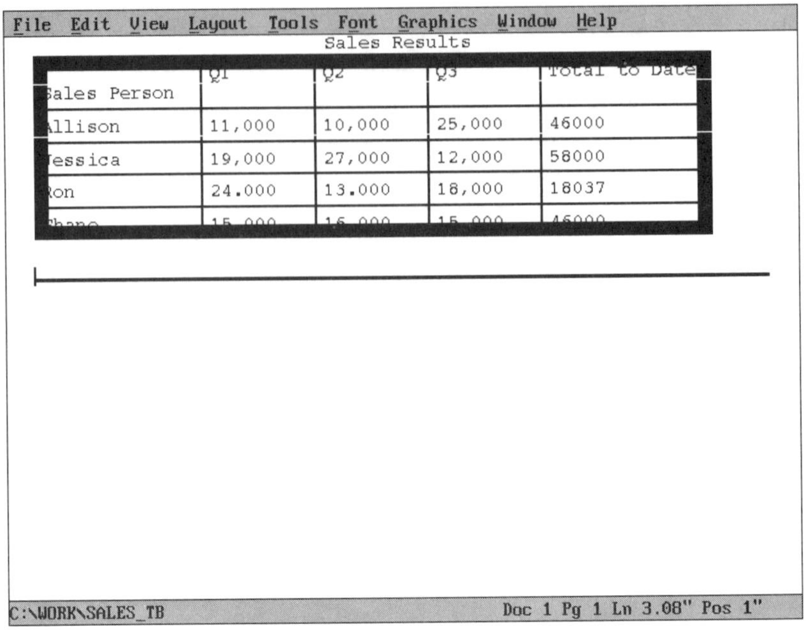

```
 File  Edit  View  Layout  Tools  Font  Graphics  Window  Help
                           Sales Results
```

Sales Person	Q1	Q2	Q3	Total to Date
Allison	11,000	10,000	25,000	46000
Jessica	19,000	27,000	12,000	58000
Ron	24.000	13.000	18,000	18037
Shane	15,000	16,000	15,000	46000

```
 C:\WORK\SALES_TB                          Doc 1 Pg 1 Ln 3.08" Pos 1"
```

Figure 6-13 It's hard to draw a line this smooth manually.

Drawing a Graphics Box If you're working on a newsletter or an overhead, a picture would make help the page get attention. Try putting one in:

1. Press Alt+g to open the *Graphics* menu, b for *Graphics Boxes,* and c for *Create.*

2. You're now going to retrieve an image that comes included with WordPerfect. In the *Create Graphics Box* window (see Figure 6-14), press f for *Filename.*

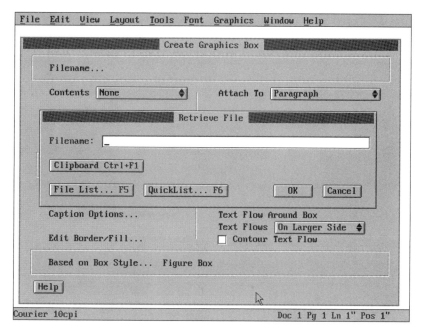

Figure 6-14 Use this window to set up your graphics box.

3. Type the name of the graphics file you want. There should be one that came with your copy of WordPerfect. In the *Retrieve File* window, type C:\WP60\TREE.WPG and press Enter.

4. Press Enter to place the image onto the screen (see Figure 6-15).

5. With the image on the screen, type this text where the cursor falls, just to the left of it:

Our foliage campaign has been highly successful so far. We all feel that we're getting a greater appreciation for the trees in our area.

Figure 6-15 You can put clip art into your documents.

Text Fits with the Picture

It can be a real trick to have text go neatly around an image in your text, but WordPerfect 6 lets you do that readily:

1. From the Graphics menu, choose *Graphics Boxes,* then *Edit.*

2. To accept the suggested box, press Enter in the *Select Box to Edit* window.

3. In the *Edit Graphics Box* window, press t for <u>T</u>ext Flow *Around Box,* then press c for <u>C</u>ontour Text Flow.

Text Fits with the Picture (continued)

4. Choose *OK.* Figure 6-16 shows the result.

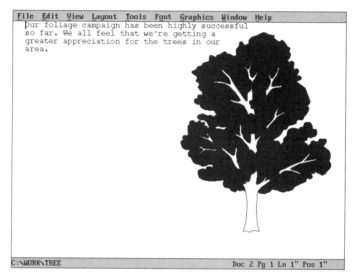

Figure 6-16 Words flow with the picture.

5. Save the file as *TREE,* and close it.

Drawing a Text Box Sometimes you may want to put text rather than pictures into boxes. In a newsletter, a box is a good way to highlight particular information:

1. In the blank document on the screen, choose Graphics, then Graphics Boxes, then Create.

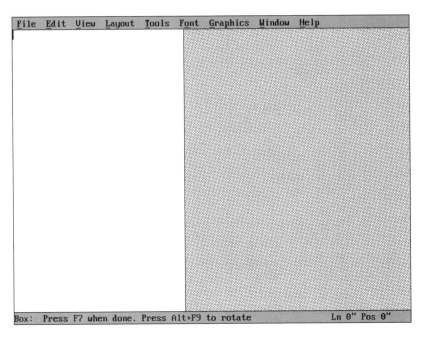

Figure 6-17 Use this for typing text in a box.

2. To prepare to type text in a box, press e for *Cr_eate Text.* A special screen appears (see Figure 6-17).

3. Type the text. Type `Eat to live, and not live to eat.` Press Enter twice, then Tab twice, and type `Benjamin Franklin.`

4. To exit, press F7, then choose *OK.* WordPerfect puts the box on the page (see Figure 6-18).

5. Close the file without saving it.

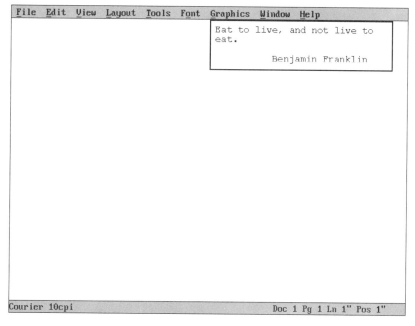

Figure 6-18 You can put text in a box on the screen.

"How Do I Draw a Box around the Whole Page?"

If you want a box around the page, you don't draw a box in the usual way. You use a special box called a *border:*

1. Using the blank document on the screen, open the Graphics menu, and choose *Borders.*

2. Choose what you want to put a border around. Choose *Page.*

3. In the *Create Page Border* window, press Enter to accept the suggested settings.

"How Do I Draw a Box around the Whole Page?" (continued)

4. To see the border, use the View menu to switch to Page Mode (see Figure 6-19).

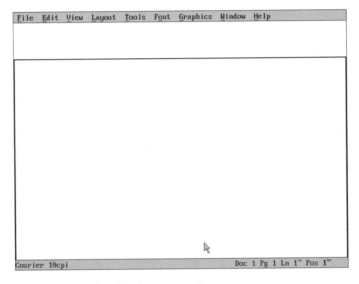

Figure 6-19 A border dresses up the page.

5. Close the file without saving it, and switch from Page Mode back to Text Mode.

Creating a Table of Contents

A table of contents is a special kind of table you often need with long reports. Typing the chapter titles into a table of contents is not really the hard part, though it is unnecessary labor. Matching text with page numbers is the true challenge to one's patience. WordPerfect automates the making of a table of contents. First, set up a document so that it has enough pages to merit a table of contents:

1. Open the document MONTH you created in Chapter 5.

2. Just to give WordPerfect a few extra pages to work with, press Ctrl+Enter just before the words *Increased Leads* (the second subhead in the report), before *Better Training Sessions,* and before *Promotions and Salary Increases.* Now the document has several pages; you can get down to the actual business of creating a table of contents.

Marking the Entries

WordPerfect needs a little bit to go on before it can make your table of contents for you. First, tell it what goes in the table by marking the entries:

1. Put the cursor in front of *Sales Last Month,* the first subhead, and press Alt+e, s, Enter to select it.

2. From the Tools menu, press b to open the *Table of Contents* submenu.

3. Now you mark the text to appear in the table. Press m for *Mark.*

4. You can have a table with main headings and subheadings, but this table will have just main headings. In the *Mark Table of Contents* window, choose *OK* to accept the level 1 for the heading in the table of contents you're creating.

5. Repeat steps 1 to 4 to mark the other subheads in the report for the table of contents—*Increased Leads, Automated Reporting, Better Training Sessions, Promotions* and *Salary Increases, and Recommendations for Advertising.*

"Hey, Thanks, Coach."

Sometimes WordPerfect goes beyond the usual Help and offers a *Coach* to lead you through an activity. Here's how you'd do it for a table of contents:

1. Press Alt+h to open the *Help* menu, then press o for *Coaches.*

"Hey, Thanks, Coach." (continued)

2. In the *Coaches* window, highlight *Create a Table of Contents,* and press Enter.

The Coach would then lead you step-by-step through creating the table. For now, though, choose *Cancel* to close the Coach window and go back to creating a table without the Coach.

Creating a Page for the Table

Having marked the entries, you have to give WordPerfect a bit more information before it can finish the job. Next, create a blank page for the table of contents:

1. Put the cursor at the top of the document and press Ctrl+Enter to put in a hard page break.

2. Press Up arrow once to put the cursor in the blank page.

Defining the Table

Once you've marked the entries, you've got to tell WordPerfect where to put the table and what format to use:

1. From the Tools menu, open the *Table of Contents* submenu, then press d for *Define.*

2. You have only one level for now, and do not need to change any other options. Press Enter to accept the suggested format and close the *Define Table of Contents* window.

Generating the Table

Having done the preparations, you can sit back and let WordPerfect automate an otherwise laborious task:

1. To generate the table of contents, choose *Generate* from the Tools menu, then, in the *Generate* window, press Enter to continue.

WordPerfect generates a nifty table of contents, complete with accurate page numbers and dots between the entries and the page numbers (see Figure 6-20).

```
File  Edit  View  Layout  Tools  Font  Graphics  Window  Help

Sales Last Month. . . . . . . . . . . . . . . . . . . . . . . . 2

Increased Leads . . . . . . . . . . . . . . . . . . . . . . . . 3

Automated Reporting . . . . . . . . . . . . . . . . . . . . . . 3

Better Training Sessions. . . . . . . . . . . . . . . . . . . . 4

Promotions and Salary Increases . . . . . . . . . . . . . . . . 5

Recommendations for Advertising . . . . . . . . . . . . . . . . 5
_____

Monthly Report

Sales Last Month

This has been a difficult month for the sales force, but we have
every reason to be optimistic about next month. It's true that
sales of our main product were down almost 25% from what they
were last year. But those figures are misleading, because we've
lowered prices so much that our increased sales don't show up as
C:\WORK\MONTH                              Doc 1 Pg 1 Ln 1.17" Pos 1"
```

Figure 6-20 WordPerfect generates a neat table of contents.

2. Save and close the document. Exit WordPerfect.

Though you won't create an index or a list in this book, you now know the fundamentals for doing them. They're the same as for a table of contents: Mark your entries, then generate the finished product.

WordPerfect may have *word* in its name, but it's not limited to working with words. You now know how to work with rows and columns, numbers, and pictures, all of which make your documents look better while saving you time and effort. There are

other ways to make life easier for yourself by setting up
WordPerfect to work the way you do, and you find out about
them in Chapter 7.

PART III

MAKING THAT PROCESSOR REALLY WHIR

Once you own something, you can do with it what you want. After Parts 1 and 2 you own WordPerfect; you can do about anything that anyone else does with it when working with your own documents. So you can enter new frontiers. Here you first find out how to set up WordPerfect to work the way you want, not the way it thinks you want. You set up the screen the way you want, control beeps and backups, and even set up a Disneyish Graphical User Interface for your mouse to cavort in (if you have a mouse.) Then you go beyond the usual WordPerfect automation to design your own automated series of steps. Finally, you perform the ultimate in hot word processing by setting up a list of addresses and using them to personalize a form letter.

CHAPTER

7

MAKING WORDPERFECT
ANTICIPATE YOUR NEEDS

109

When you first started using WordPerfect, it was probably enough just to be able to get things done its way. Telling WordPerfect how to work was out of the question. Not that you've used it for awhile, though, you've found out how it works and how you work as you use it. You can change WordPerfect around to get it to anticipate your needs.

Making a Permanent Default Directory

In Chapter 4 you saw how to set up a directory that would be your main (default) directory until you shut down WordPerfect for the day. If you wanted to have that directory be your default the next time, though, you'd have to repeat the steps. You can set up WordPerfect so that you don't have to run through those steps each time:

1. Start WordPerfect, display the File menu, and press t to choose the *Setup* submenu (see Figure 7-1).

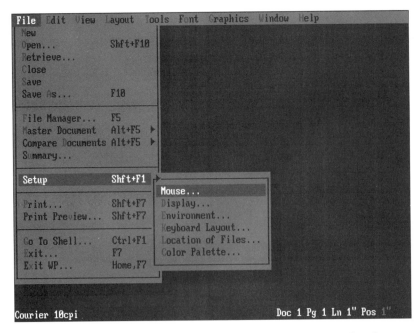

Figure 7-1 Use the Setup menu to change the look of WordPerfect.

2. You want to change where WordPerfect locates files. Press 1 for *Location of Files.*

3. *In the Location of Files* window (see Figure 7-2), press d for *Documents.*

4. Type your permanent default directory. In the box that appears, type C:\WORK. Whenever you want to open a file, WordPerfect will suggest starting in C:\WORK. When you want to save a file, it will save it there unless you specify somewhere else. Best of all, it will continue to treat C:\WORK as your main directory even after you exit from WordPerfect and restart it.

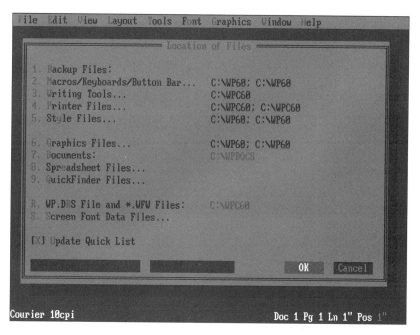

Figure 7-2 Here you regulate where WordPerfect keeps various files.

"I Forget the Name of the Directory I Want."

When you want to type in your permanent directory in the section *Making a Permanent Default Directory*, you might not remember the exact name of the directory you want to type in, or you may not be sure if you still have it:

1. After you choose the File menu, then Setup, then Location of Files, and then Documents, press F8 for *Directory Tree* in the box that appears. WordPerfect shows you the *Directory Tree* window.

2. Highlight the name of the directory you want to work with, and press Enter. The name of the highlighted directory appears next to *Documents*. Then choose *OK* to close the Location of Files window.

Getting the Screen the Way You Want It

Changing screen modes is the most noticeable way to change the look of the screen. In earlier chapters you've worked in Text Mode, Graphics Mode, and Page Mode; and you've seen how the screen changes for each one. Other changes are not quite so dramatic, but they can make the screen suit the way you work.

Changing Screen Colors

The basic colors on your screen work just fine, so there's no purely practical reason to change the colors. You may find another set of colors more pleasing, or you may want to change colors from time to time for the same reason you rearrange your living room furniture occasionally:

1. Display the File menu and then the Setup menu, and press d for *Display*.

2. To work with your colors, in the *Display* window, press t for *Text Mode Screen Type/Colors*.

3. In the *Text Mode Screen Type/Colors* window (see Figure 7-3), press c for *Color Schemes.*

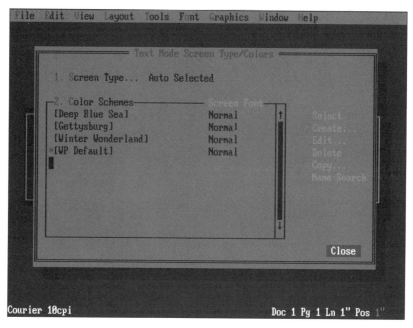

Figure 7-3 You can choose from these poetically named color schemes.

4. Choose a different color scheme. Highlight *[Winter Wonderland]*, and press s for *Select*, then press Enter to close the Display window.

The screen takes on the new color scheme, as will windows and boxes when you open them. Even though figure 7-4 is in black and white, you can tell from the light background that the colors have changed.

5. Repeat the steps, but in step five select *[WP Default]* to restore the standard WordPerfect colors.

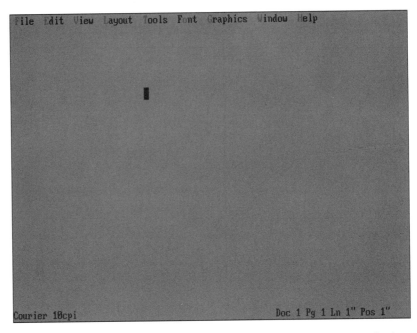

File Edit View Layout Tools Font Graphics Window Help

Courier 10cpi   Doc 1 Pg 1 Ln 1" Pos 1"

Figure 7-4 Sometimes it wakes you up to see the screen in a fresh color.

Designing Your Own Windows

You already know from Chapter 3 how to have two windows open on the screen at once. There are some other ways you can remodel your windows to make them more useful, such as putting a frame around them or rearranging them on the screen so you can see several of them at once. First, add a frame:

Press Alt+w to open the *Window* menu, then press f for *Frame.* A two-line frame appears around the window you're working in. See Figure 7-5.

Windows are particularly useful when you're working with more than one document, but you may want to be able to see more than one window at once:

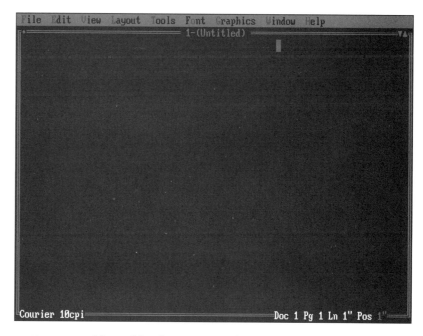

Figure 7-5 If you like frames around you windows, you can have them.

Press Shift+F10 twice to open two more blank documents. The newest document will say *Doc 3* in the lower right.

Now rearrange the windows:

So you can see all three at once, display the Window menu and press t for *Tile.*

It's often useful to switch quickly between two windows. One might have your notes from a conversation and the other one the final write up. Or one might have a rough draft and the other a final draft.

To switch from the current window to the previous window, press Shift+F3.

Try some more maneuvers:

1. To get to the next window, choose *Next* from the Window menu. Continue to choose *Next* until you are in the window that says *Doc 1* in the lower right.

2. To *Minimize* the current window (make it a small size), press i. Figure 7-6 shows the minimized window.

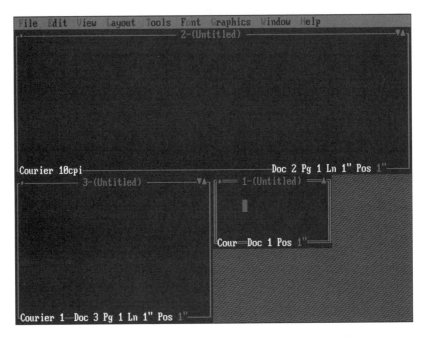

Figure 7-6 Minimize a window if you want to see it but don't want it taking up much of the screen.

3. To restore it to full size, choose *Maximize* from the Window menu. The window then takes up the whole screen.

4. To close the extra windows, switch to each one and choose *Close* from the File menu. Stop when only the window for document 1 remains.

Getting Rid of the Status Message

The message in the lower left of the screen tells you which font you're using or warns you when you're in Typeover mode instead of Insert mode. You can take it right off the screen if you don't use it:

1. Open the View menu and choose *Screen Setup.*

2. In the *Screen Setup* window (See Figure 7-7), press w for *Window Options.*

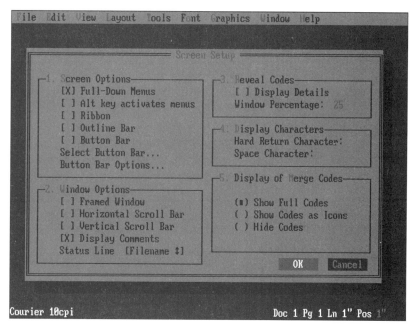

Figure 7-7 Here you control all kinds of things about your screen.

3. To remove the line, press s for *Status Line*, then n for *Nothing* and choose *OK.* The status message goes away.

4. To restore the message, repeat the steps and choose *Filename* in step 3.

"Say It Didn't Happen. I Lost My Menus."

When you redecorate, sometimes you face problems you hadn't reckoned on. For instance, you can elect to work without menus, a nice way to create more blank space on the screen, but there's a hitch to it. Once the menus are gone, you can't use menus for anything, not even to get your menus back. It's like locking up the controls to your car and not having a key to unlock them. Nobody else can fiddle with them, but neither can you.

Getting rid of menus is easy enough:

Open the View menu, and press p for *Pull-Down Menus.* Just like that, your menus are gone (see Figure 7-8). But you can't open the View menu to get them back, because it isn't there any more:

Doc 1 Pg 1 Ln 1" Pos 1"

Figure 7-8 The screen is streamlined without menus . . . but harder to use.

"Say It Didn't Happen. I Lost My Menus." (continued)

1. To get the menus back when they're not displayed, press Alt+= (Alt plus the equals sign, in the top right of the keyboard.) The menus come back, but still only temporarily; you'd lose them if you exited WordPerfect.

2. To make them permanent, display the View menu and press p for *Pull-Down Menus.* The menus are back to stay.

Silencing Beeps and Regulating Backups

Certain things take place in the background, and you might not expect to be able to do much about them, but you can take control in the case of beeps from the computer and automatic backups of your work.

Keeping WordPerfect Silent

Traditionally, computers have beeped to alert people to errors. WordPerfect doesn't do that, and it's just as well. If you want the beeps, though, you can have them:

1. Display the File menu and then the Setup submenu.

2. To work with such things as beeps, press e for *Environment* (see Figure 7-9), then press e for *Beep Options.*

If you wanted beeps, you'd press the letters for the beep options you wanted. For now, though, don't put the options into place.

3. Select *Cancel* to close the window without putting in more beeps. Without closing the *Environment* window, look over a couple other possibilities.

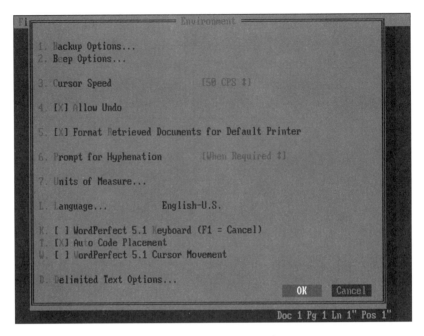

Figure 7-9 Here you control beeps and much more.

Regulating Backups

On a typewriter, a power failure would never be a serious danger to your work. When the power came back on, you'd start right in wherever you had left off on the page. If a power failure were to strike your word processor, though, you'd lose all the work you hadn't saved to disk.

WordPerfect protects you. If there is a failure, it automatically saves your open documents to backup files. Then, when you restarted WordPerfect, you'd see a message like the one in Figure 7-10.

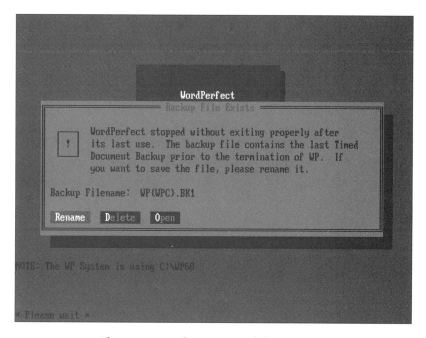

Figure 7-10 If you restart after a power failure, you get a chance to recover your file.

You can choose whether or not to have WordPerfect make the automatic backup:

1. In the Environment window (still open from the previous steps), press b for *Backup Options.* If you didn't want the automatic backup, you'd remove the X from the box in front of *Timed Document Backup,* but leave it for now.

2. Press Esc to leave the *Backup* window without changing the default settings.

3. Choose *Cancel* to close the Environment window.

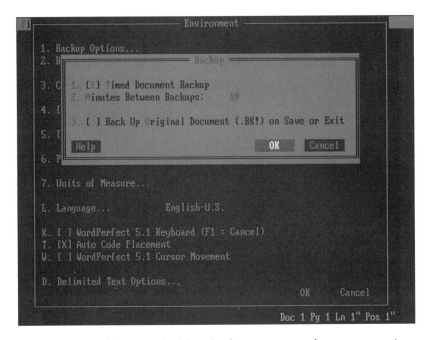

Figure 7-11 You can decide whether or not to have automatic backups.

Training Your Mouse to Dance

Most people who use WordPerfect probably don't use a mouse, and you can do anything with the keyboard you can do with the mouse. Most of the time the keyboard's quicker anyway, because your hands are already on it, and you can just tap away.

In WordPerfect 6, though, mouse users can have more fun, and they can do some things easier than people who don't have a mouse.

> **Read This If You're Left-Handed.**
>
> To make your mouse left-handed (so that the right button is the main button, instead of the left,) you would again use setup. You'd display the File menu and the Setup submenu,

Read This If You're Left-Handed.

then press m to open the *Mouse* submenu, shown in Figure 7-12. You'd press 1 to put an X in front of *Left-handed Mouse,* and you'd choose OK. If you're right-handed but just wanted to look at the *Mouse* window, press Esc to leave the window without changing any settings.

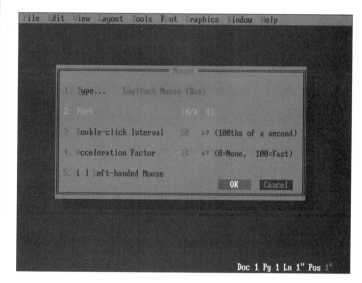

Figure 7-12 Here you can make your mouse left-or right-handed.

Putting in Scroll Bars

You may know that Microsoft Windows programs, Macintosh programs, and other programs designed for use with a mouse have a feature called *scroll bars* that you use to move around in the document. In WordPerfect 6, you too can have scroll bars:

1. To get a bar across the bottom, choose the View menu, and press h for *Horizontal Scroll Bar.*

2. To get a bar along the right side, again choose the View
menu, and this time press v for *Vertical Scroll Bar.* Figure 7-
13 shows the screen with both vertical and horizontal scroll
bars.

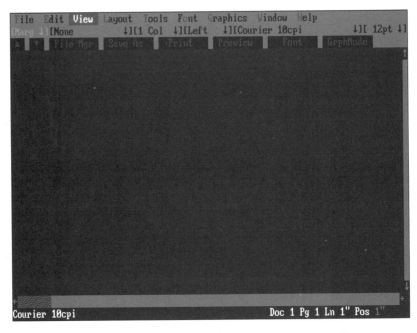

Figure 7-13 Now WordPerfect offers on-screen tools for mouse
users.

To use the scroll bars to move through a document, first you'd
have to have a document on the screen. Then you'd click on the
arrows at the ends of the bars. For example, to move down a line at
a time, you'd click again and again on the down arrow at the
bottom of the vertical scroll bar. To scroll continuously through a
document, you'd put the mouse pointer over an arrow on the scroll
bar and hold down the mouse button.

Displaying a Ribbon and Button Bar

You may have heard the term *Graphical User Interface*; in this section you're finding what that's all about: You point at various graphical images on the screen instead of typing commands. For mouse users there are additional graphical tools, besides the scroll bars, they can use instead of typing commands. You can put in a *Ribbon* and a *Button Bar:*

1. To place a Ribbon across the top of the screen, choose the View menu and press r for *Ribbon* (see Figure 7-13).

2. To put a Button Bar across the top of the screen, choose the View menu and press b for *Button Bar.*

To use the ribbon or the button bar, you point to what you want, then click. Try it:

1. Put the mouse pointer on top of *Courier 10cpi* in the Ribbon, and click. A menu of additional fonts drops down. To choose one, you'd point to the one you wanted and click again.

2. To close the drop down menu, click on any blank space on the screen.

Now try the button bar, where you also point and click:

1. Click on *File Mgr* on the button bar. The *Specify File Manager List* window comes up, just as it would if you pressed F5 from the keyboard.

2. Press Esc to close the *File Manager List* window without using it.

3. To remove the Scroll Bars, the Ribbon, and the Button Bar from the screen, repeat the steps you followed to open them.

Using the Outline Tool

WordPerfect can also anticipate some of your needs when you create an outline. Creating an outline on your own can be tricky: You have to be careful to keep the numbering consistent in all your headings and subheads, for one thing, and you have to keep the indentation uniform. With WordPerfect's Outline tool, though, you can focus on what goes into the outline. WordPerfect does the tedious formatting for you.

Creating an Outline

The biggest step in creating an outline with WordPerfect is telling WordPerfect that you want to create one. Then it does all it can to help you. First, tell WordPerfect that you want to do it:

1. From the Tools menu, choose *Outline,* then, to indicate that you want to create an outline, choose *Begin New Outline* from the *Outline* submenu (see Figure 7-14).

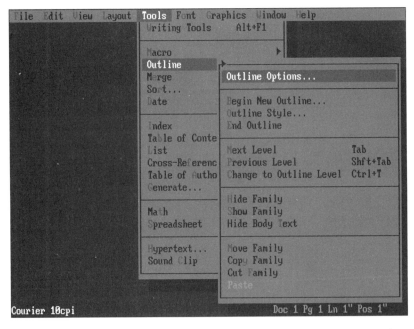

Figure 7-14 With this menu you do all kinds of things with outlines.

2. In the *Outline Style List* window (see Figure 7-15), highlight *Outline* and, to select it and close the window, press s.

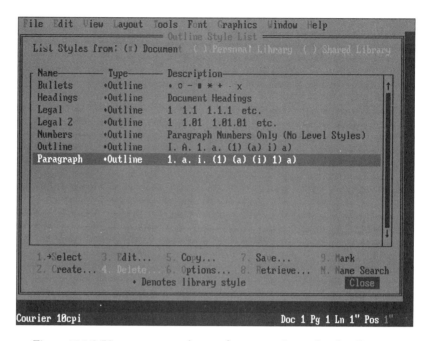

Figure 7-15 Here you can choose from a variety of styles for your outline.

Now WordPerfect assists you in preparing an outline. Notice that a Roman numeral I is already in the top left. Type the first heading:

1. Type `Marketing Plan`, and press Enter. A Roman numeral II appears for you to type the next header.

2. Type three additional headers, and press Enter after each one: `Advertising Plan`, `Financial Organization`, and `Special Considerations`. Figure 7-16 shows the outline with these four main heads.

Of course, an outline has other levels besides main heads. Add a second level of headings, and watch WordPerfect take care of numbering and indentation:

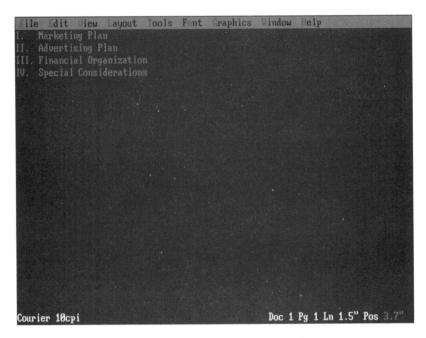

Figure 7-16 WordPerfect worries about the numbering as you type the headings.

1. Put the cursor at the end of the words *Marketing Plan,* and press Enter to put the cursor on the next line. Don't worry about the roman numeral II at the left. Here's how to change the main head to a subhead.

2. Press Tab. WordPerfect indents the text and puts in the letter *A.* Type `Special Programs`, and press Enter. A letter *B* appears on the left for the next subhead. Type `Sales Training`.

3. Repeat steps 1 and 2 to put two subheads under *Advertising Plan.* For the A subhead, type `Mass Mailings`. For the B subhead, type `Newspapers`.

You've created an outline, and your only concern is what to put into it. You let WordPerfect take care of the rest.

Working with the Outline

Outlines are often for planning, and the power of WordPerfect's automated outliner shows up when you work with it in various ways. Suppose, for one thing, you wanted to add a text note that did not follow the outline format. Here's how to do so:

> Put the cursor at the end of the outline, after *Special Considerations*, and press Enter to move to a new line. To get rid of the Roman numeral and type *Body Text* instead, open the Tools menu, choose *Outline*, then choose *Change to Body Text*. You're free to type in the usual mode, without having outline numbers pop in when you don't want them. Type `That's our preliminary outline. We will be submitting it next week.`

Next, try inserting a fresh heading, and watch as WordPerfect renumbers for you:

> Put the cursor after *Mass Mailings*, and press Enter. Notice that a capital B appears, and the former B topic becomes a C topic. Type in the new heading—`Handouts`.

Now put in a new main heading:

1. Put the cursor after *Newspapers,* and press Enter. Press Shift+Tab. The letter *D* changes to a Roman numeral III.

2. Type `Management Team`.

If you want to edit the outline in more ambitious ways, WordPerfect has an *Outline Editing Mode* to help you.:

1. Move the cursor to the top of the outline. From the Tools menu, choose *Outline,* then *Outline Options*. In the Outline window, type `t` to choose *Edit in Outline Mode*. A special Outline menu appears across the top of the screen beneath the usual menu, and the first subhead and all its subheads are highlighted (see Figure 7-17).

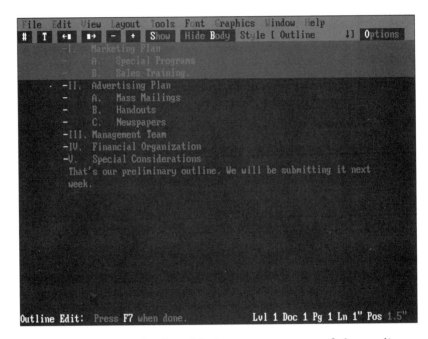

Figure 7-17 Use Outline Mode to move parts of the outline around.

From here it's easy to move outline items around.

2. Press the down arrow three times, until you've highlighted the second family—*Advertising Plan* and its subheads.

3. To choose the options available as you edit, press o to choose *Options* from the Outline menu. The Outline window appears (see Figure 7-18).

4. To move the highlighted family, press m for *Move Family,* then press Enter. The highlighted family goes to the clipboard, so you can't see it on the screen for a moment.

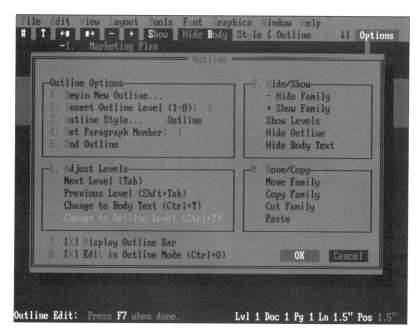

Figure 7-18 Use this window to work with an outline when you're using Outline Mode.

5. To put the family in the new position, press the up arrow to move to the top of the document, then press Enter. *Advertising Plan* and its subheadings appears in the new position.

Collapsing and Expanding an Outline

When working with an outline you often want to drop back at times and get the big picture by seeing just your main headings. At other times you may want to see all the detail at once. Here's how to collapse and expand the outline:

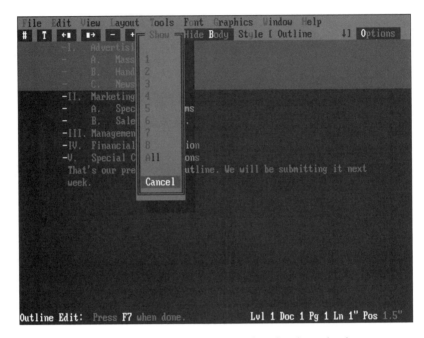

Figure 7-19 Here choose how many outline levels to display.

1. While still in Outline Edit, press s to open the *Show* window (see Figure 7-19), then press 1. Only the main headings display.

2. Repeat step one and choose *All* to display the whole outline.

3. Press F7 to leave Outline Edit mode.

"Oh, For a Mouse at a Time Like This"

When you're in Outline Edit mode, you don't need a mouse to work with the Outline menu. You can press the highlighted letters and symbols in the menu at the top, such as *o* for *Options* or *s* for *Show*. Even in Outline Edit, it's easier to point with a mouse pointer and click than to use the keyboard. Once you're not using Outline Edit mode, you have to go back to it to take editing shortcuts for things like moving a family. If you have a mouse, though, you can use

"Oh For a Mouse at a Time Like This" (continued)

the special outlining menu any time you want:

Display the View menu, then press o for *Outline Bar.* The special outlining menu appears at the top again. You need to use a mouse with it, and then you can get the benefits of using the Outline menu even when you aren't in Outline Edit mode.

Once you know WordPerfect well enough to have some idea of how you might want to change it, you have tools at your fingertips to do just that. You can make life easier for yourself in other ways, too. In the next chapter you find out how to set up one command for carrying out a series of steps that you do often.

CHAPTER
8

TYPING THINGS ONCE, THEN USING THEM OVER AND OVER

WordPerfect has done its best to figure out what you're going to want to do, and has created menus of commands for all those things. But WordPerfect can't anticipate everything, so it allows you to create commands of your own, called macros. Because you have to set them up, you could say that macros are like the push buttons on your car radio. The radio can remember stations you want to use, but it's up to you to tell it what to remember.

Styles are another way to save yourself time and trouble. By assigning styles to paragraphs, you format them without having to put in all the formatting codes yourself. Later, if you change the style, you change it for all paragraphs in that style.

Storing Keystrokes You Use a Lot

Macros don't have to be something complicated. Maybe there's a word or phrase you have to type over and over again. You can create a macro so that, instead of typing the phrase, you can just play the macro. Suppose you were writing an advertising brochure that made frequent reference to *the sound-proof stealth helicopter from Meyers' Associates.* You could put the phrase into a macro so that you wouldn't have to type it over and over, and so you'd be sure of typing it correctly:

1. To start recording the macro, press Alt+t to open the Tools menu, m for *Macro,* then r for *Record.*

2. In the *Record Macro* window, type the name `copter`, and press Enter. The words *Recording Macro* appear at the bottom left of the screen (see Figure 8-1).

3. Back in the document, type the macro: `the sound-proof stealth helicopter from Meyers' Associates.`

4. To stop recording, press Alt+t to open the Tools menu, m for *Macro,* then s for *Stop.* You've recorded the macro. It's ready for you to use.

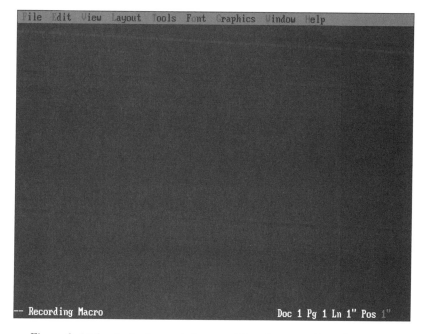

Figure 8-1 Check the lower left to see if you're recording the macro.

Putting the Stored Keystrokes into Use

Now that you've stored the keystrokes, you can just play the macro any time you want to use them. Try playing back the macro:

1. Choose *Macro* from the Tools menu, and this time press p to play the macro.

2. To identify which macro to play, in the *Play Macro* window, type COPTER, and press Enter. The phrase appears in the document. See Figure 8-2.

3. Save the document with the name *Ad.*

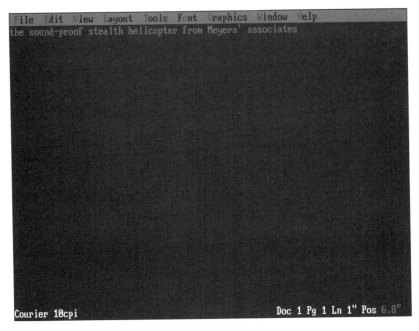

```
 File  Edit  View  Layout  Tools  Font  Graphics  Window  Help
the sound-proof stealth helicopter from Meyers' associates




















Courier 10cpi                                    Doc 1 Pg 1 Ln 1" Pos 6.8"
```

Figure 8-2 When you play the macro, the keystrokes appear in the document.

"It's Hard to Remember the Name of the Macro."

If you use a macro a lot, you can record it in a special way so that you don't even have to type the name of it. You'll be able to play it back by pressing Alt and a single key. Suppose, for instance, you wanted to have a key combination for saving a file, so you wouldn't have to choose Save from the menu:

1. To start recording display the Tools menu and choose *Macro* and *Record,* just as for any other macro.

2. To code the macro to work with the Alt key, in the *Record Macro* window, press Alt+s, and press Enter to close the window.

"It's Hard to Remember the Name of the Macro."

3. Back in the document, record the steps to save a document: Press Alt+f, then s.

4. To stop recording, display the Tools menu, choose *Macro* and choose *Stop*.

The joy of macros it not in recording them but in using them over and over again once you've done so. You've recorded the macro for saving using the Alt key; try playing it back:

1. Press the Alt key combination you've set up—Alt+s. WordPerfect saves the file.

2. Close the file you've been working with.

Macros take only a few moments to record and just an instant to play back. For anything you find yourself doing over and over again, consider using a macro to save yourself the tedium. If you often block out a word and then italicize it, for example, make a macro for Alt+i so you can do it in one stroke. Always print to the same printer? Make a macro Alt+p to do it for you; Alt+p for print is easier to remember than the actual shortcut keys for printing, Shift+F7. And, in your macro, you could include all the steps so that the one macro fills in the Print window and sets the document to printing.

Using Formatting Over and Over

In fashion, styles are a way to dress up the ordinary. WordPerfect offers styles of its own, as a way to dress up text. The styles are stored formatting to help you make titles, headings, and subheadings look just like those from the professionals.

Applying Styles

Though you could create styles of your own, you can benefit from them without even taking the time to store your own special set of keystrokes. WordPerfect provides several predesigned styles:

1. To apply one of WordPerfect's styles to existing text, first open the document named *MONTH* that you created and saved in an earlier chapter.

2. To say which paragraph to apply styles to, put the cursor anywhere in the subhead, *Sales Last Month.*

3. Now find the style. Press Alt+l to open the *Layout* menu and s to open the *Styles* submenu.

4. In the *Style List* window, highlight *Level 1* (see Figure 8-3), and press s to *Select* it. The title takes on the stored formatting, with a numeral at the start of the line (see Figure 8-4).

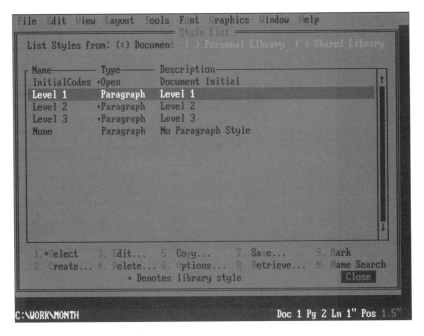

Figure 8-3 Use the Style List to assign styles.

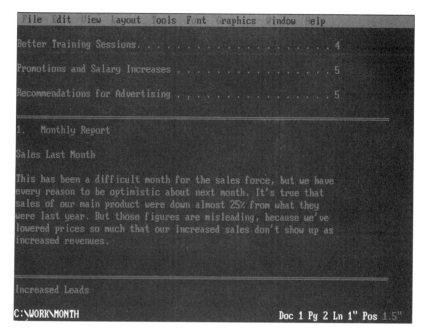

File Edit View Layout Tools Font Graphics Window Help

Better Training Sessions. 4

Promotions and Salary Increases 5

Recommendations for Advertising 5

1.   Monthly Report

Sales Last Month

This has been a difficult month for the sales force, but we have
every reason to be optimistic about next month. It's true that
sales of our main product were down almost 25% from what they
were last year. But those figures are misleading, because we've
lowered prices so much that our increased sales don't show up as
increased revenues.

Increased Leads

C:\WORK\MONTH   Doc 1 Pg 2 Ln 1" Pos 1.5"

Figure 8-4 Styles put the line in a standard style.

Follow similar steps to format another subhead in *MONTH:*

Put the cursor in the subhead *Increased Leads,* choose *Styles* from the Layout menu, and again select *Level 1.* You could continue to apply the style to the other subheads.

With at least two subheads set up in the same style, you're ready to see in the next section perhaps the greatest benefit of styles: When you change the style for one paragraph, you change it for all the paragraphs in that style.

Changing a Style Once to Change It Everywhere

You might wonder why it's worth the trouble to put paragraphs into a particular style. After all, you could quite quickly format each paragraph in that style and be done with it. The benefit shows up when you change a style. Suppose you wanted to put the the Level 1 subheads in Monthly Report into bold typeface:

1. From the Layout menu, open the Style List window.

2. To change a heading you have in place in the document, highlight *Level 1,* and press e for *Edit,* then, in the *Edit Style* window, press 4 for *Style Contents.*

3. Using the list at the top of the window to show you which keys to use, Press Ctrl+F8 to change the font.

4. Press 3 for *Appearance* and 1 for *Bold.*

5. Choose *OK* to go back to the Edit Style, where the Style Contents window now shows the code *[Bold On]* at the beginning of the line (see Figure 8-5).

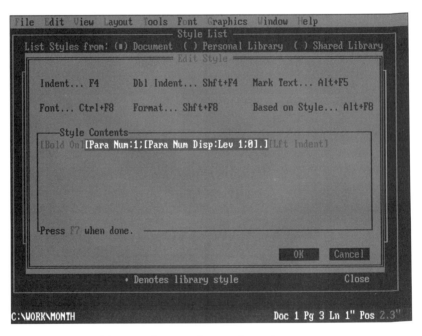

Figure 8-5 Add a code here to change the style.

6. Press F7 to close the Edit Style window, then choose OK. Close the Style List window. All headings in the Level 1 style are now in bold (see Figure 8-6). If you had fifteen headings, you'd change them all with a single style change instead of having to change each one individually.

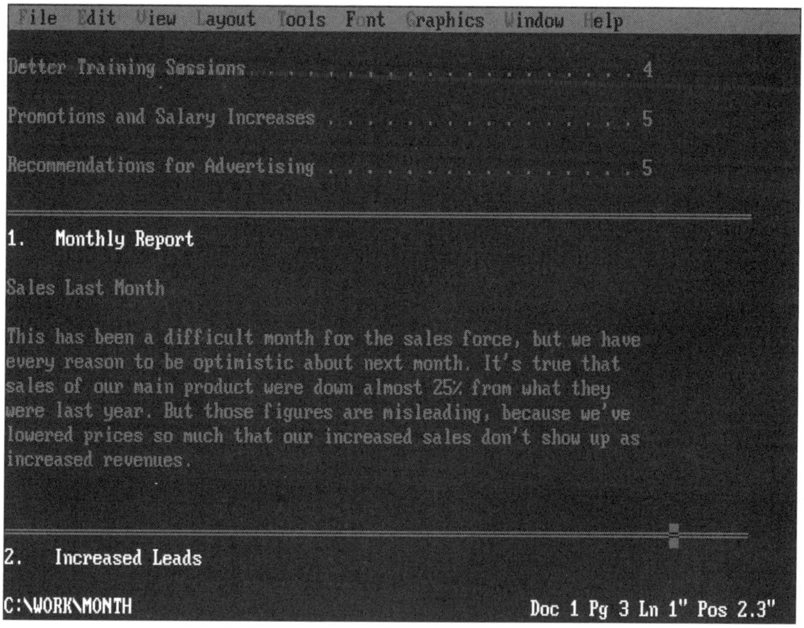

Figure 8-6 When you change a style, you change all text in that style.

"Oh, No, I've Ruined the Style."

When you change codes as you did in the previous steps, it's easy to delete a code accidentally or add another code you decide you don't want. When working with codes, things can get complicated quite quickly, but don't worry. Style changes you make take effect only in the document you're working on. The WordPerfect styles remain unchanged and will be the same as before whenever you use them in a different document.

There's almost no end, it seems, to the ways you can automate your work in WordPerfect. What WordPerfect hasn't automated for you already, you can automate for yourself using macros. With styles, you can save yourself the trouble of formatting titles, headings, and subheads, and be confident of a professional look as you do it. In the next chapter you'll see the highest form of automation in WordPerfect—using mail merge to type a letter just once yet personalize it for a whole list of people.

CHAPTER

9

TYPING A LETTER JUST ONCE, THEN USING IT OVER AND OVER

Everybody gets personalized mailings these days. Ed McMahon writes a letter saying you've won a million dollars in a sweepstakes, and your own name is in large print right on the envelope. It's inside on the letter as well. Not everybody knows how to create personalized form letters, but you can do it with WordPerfect.

Suppose, for instance, you decided to send copies of the *Summer Fun Fest* flyer you created earlier to several offices for posting. You can write the letter just once yet have each letter talk personally to someone at each office.

Creating the Mailing List

First you'll create the mailing list containing codes for things like people's names and addresses as well as a number of specific names and addresses. After that you'll create one letter and put those codes in it. In the grand finale, when you merge the two, you get a personalized letter for each name and address in your mailing list.

Start by creating the list of coded names and addresses:

1. Type `Sara Campbell`, the name of the first person on your list.

2. Now create a code to go with the name. Choose the Tools menu, then, to open the *Merge* submenu, press e. To define details about the code, press d for *Define*. The *Merge Codes* window opens (see Figure 9-1), where you tell WordPerfect whether the document is text or a table.

3. To indicate that the document is text, press d for *Data [Text]*. A window opens with codes for a text document, the *Merge Codes (Text Data File)* window (see Figure 9-2).

4. Select the code for ending a field. Press f for *End Field*. (The name is one *field*. There will be several others. Together, the fields will make up a *record*.) WordPerfect puts the code *ENDFIELD* right after *Sara,* and the cursor goes to the next line.

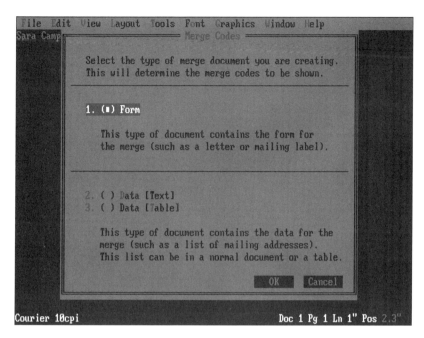

Figure 9-1 Here tell whether your document is text or a table.

You have one field, for Sara's name; now do some other fields, one for her branch office, one for her address, and one for her first name:

1. Type `Winfield Branch` and, to put in the code to end the field, press F9.

2. To put in a two-line field for the address, followed by a code, type `309 Center Circle`, and press Enter. (Don't put a code after the first line of the address.) On the next line type `Winfield, NY 13354` and press F9 for the code. Finally, put in a nickname, `Happy`, and press F9 for *ENDFIELD*.

You've typed in all the fields, so it's time to put in a code to end the record:

1. Display the Tools menu, and press e for *Merge* and d for *Define*.

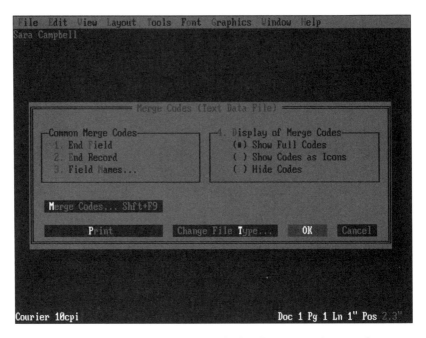

Figure 9-2 Here you choose the code for the text you've typed.

2. This time, from the Merge Codes (Text Data File) window, press e for *End Record.* WordPerfect puts in an ENDRECORD code and a hard page return (see Figure 9-3).

3. Save the file with the name *ADDRESS.*

Adding Names and Addresses

Mail merge becomes useful when you are working with multiple addresses, so type in some more addresses:

1. Follow the same steps you followed in *Creating the Mailing List* to add these additional records to the data file:

```
Dolores Reese

Highland Branch

44 Oracle Place

Oldman, NY 13548
```

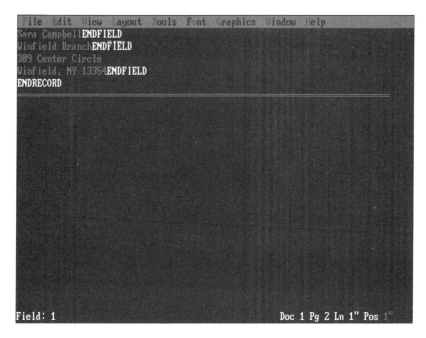

```
File  Edit  View  Layout  Tools  Font  Graphics  Window  Help
Sara CampbellENDFIELD
Winfield BranchENDFIELD
309 Center Circle
Winfield, NY 13354ENDFIELD
ENDRECORD




Field: 1                                          Doc 1 Pg 2 Ln 1" Pos 1"
```

Figure 9-3 One complete record with several fields.

Dot

Tom Stellar

City Center

2536 Central St.

Colonial, NY 13259

Butch

Tina Louise

Eastern Branch

4900 East Louisiana

Harbridge, NY 13354

Tin

Steve Miskin

Indian Grounds

```
21 Lexington

Avery, NY 13266

Flash
```

2. You don't need the hard page break after the final record, so press Backspace to delete it.

Creating the Form Letter

The codes in the data file only have meaning when there's a form file to go with them. You use the form file to generate letters one after the other that substitute the names in the data file for codes in the form file.

Telling WordPerfect that It's a Form File

To be able to perform the merge later, you have to let WordPerfect know that the file is a *form file* (one to use in a merge). To begin to create the form letter, define it:

1. Open a new document by pressing Alt+f, then n.

2. Open the Tools menu and the Merge submenu and press d for *Define*. With *Form* already highlighted, press Enter to define the file as a Form File.

Putting in a Date Code

In this form letter you'll put in two kinds of codes—a date code for putting the current date into the letter, and field codes that WordPerfect will use to substitute information from the data file for the codes:

1. To begin assigning codes to the Form File, press Shift+F9 to choose *Merge Codes* from the *Merge Codes (Form File)* window (see Figure 9-4).

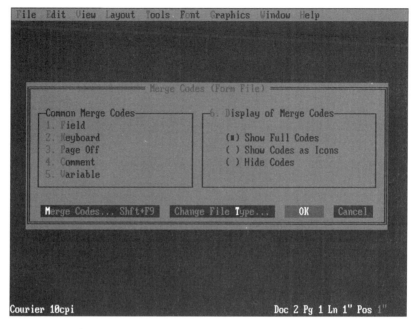

Figure 9-4 Use the Merge Codes (Form File) window to put codes in the form letter.

> 2. Highlight *DATE* in the *All Merge Codes* window (see Figure 9-5), and press Enter to select it. WordPerfect puts a *DATE* code at the top of the page, so that WordPerfect will put the current date at the top of each letter.

Putting in Merge Codes and Typing the Text

As you type the letter, you put in codes for information like name and address instead of putting in the actual information. Later, you'll use the codes to generate letters to individuals:

> 1. To put blank lines after the date, press Enter four times.
>
> 2. To put in the first code, for the person's name, from the Tools menu, choose *Merge, Define, Field.*

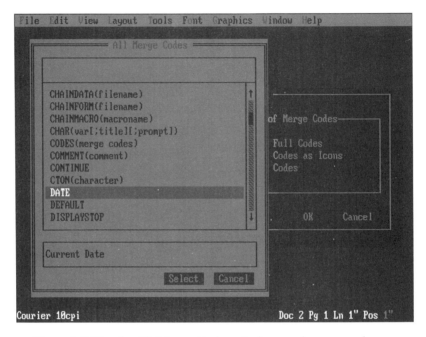

Figure 9-5 Use the All Merge Codes window to choose a code.

3. In the *Parameter Entry* window for the field (see Figure 9-6), choose *List Field Names* by pressing F5 to help you find the field name.

4. In the *Select Data File For Field Names* window, type ADDRESS (the name of the file you created in Creating the Mailing List above.)

5. In the *List Field Names* window, highlight *001 Sara Campbell,* and press Enter. To put the code into the letter, choose *OK* in the Parameter Entry window.

You've put in a code for first name, now put in a code for address:

1. Press Enter once to move to the next line below *FIELD(001),* and repeat steps 2 to 4 to get to the List Field Names window.

2. To put in the address code, highlight code *003,* and press Enter. Press Enter again to put the code into the letter.

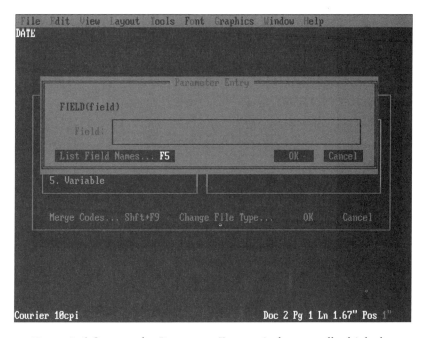

Figure 9-6 Start at the Parameter Entry window to tell which data fields to use.

So far the letter is just a collection of codes (see Figure 9-7). You still have to type the text of the letter to contain the codes.

1. Press Enter twice, then type Dear and press the spacebar once to start the letter. You're ready to put in a code for the nickname.

2. Repeat the steps to put in a code, and this time, in the List Field Names window highlight *004 Happy,* and press Enter twice to put the code into the letter. Type a comma to follow the salutation, and press enter twice.

3. Begin to type the text of the letter, as follows:

After months of talking, we've completed all the arrangements for the summer fun fest. We're looking forward to seeing everyone from the.

You're ready to put a code into the text of the letter, for the name of the office.

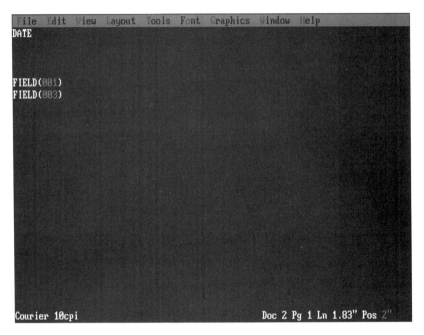

Figure 9-7 Here's the letter with just codes, before you put in text.

4. Put a space after *the* and, to put in the code for the office, repeat the steps to put in a code and choose *002* from the List Field Names window.

5. Press the spacebar once and continue the text of the letter with the words `office at our little get together.`

`Please post the enclosed flyer somewhere prominent.`
`Feel free to make copies, of course.`

`Thanks,`

6. After *Thanks,* put in the code for the nickname by repeating the steps to put in a code and choosing *004* again.

7. Press Enter twice, and type the closing, `Looking forward to the fun` followed by a comma. Leave the name blank, so you can sign it personally.

8. Save the form file as *FORMLTR.* Figure 9-8 shows the completed form letter.

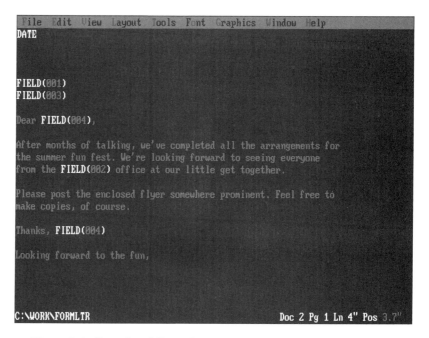

Figure 9-8 Completed Form Letter.

Merging the List and the Letter

It may take some extra time to set up the data file and the form letter the first time. Once you have them, though, you save yourself all kinds of time later. You can use the addresses and names over and over for various form letters you might create.

Once you've got the data file and the form file, you have the fun of watching automation do your work for you as you perform the merge:

1. Open a fresh document, then, from the Tools menu, choose *Merge,* then *Run.*

2. In the *Run Merge* window (see Figure 9-9), you identify the Form File and Data File. Press F5 and choose *FORMLTR* for the Form File, then press F5 and choose *ADDRESS* for the Data File.

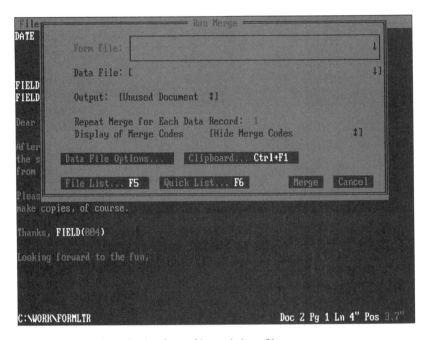

Figure 9-9 Identify the form file and data file.

3. To choose *Merge* from the commands at the bottom of the window, press Enter.

WordPerfect creates as many copies of the letter as there are addresses in the form file. Figure 9-10 shows the completed merge document, which contains five letters. To print the letters, you'd save it and print the document the same as you would any other WordPerfect document. Each letter would print on a separate page.

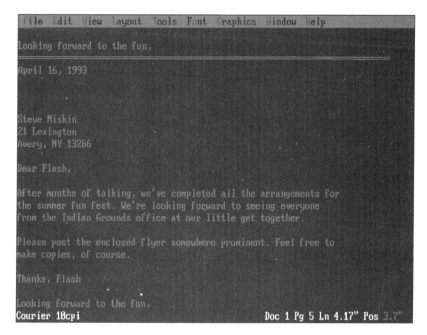

Figure 9-10 Merge replaces codes with real information.

Not everyone performs merges with WordPerfect, even if they've been using it for some time. If you're driving a BMW with lots of horsepower, though, it's tempting now and then to take it out on a lonely stretch of road and open it up. If you're using WordPerfect, it's also tempting to set it up so that it can really do a lot of work for you while you do nothing. It does just that for you when you perform a merge. You're familiar with WordPerfect now and ready to do about anything with it on your own.

APPENDIX

A

INSTALLING WORDPERFECT

To use WordPerfect on your computer, you have to transfer it from the set of floppy disks it comes on to the hard disk on your computer.

Reviewing the Equipment You Need

If you have an IBM PC or compatible, then you probably have what you need to run WordPerfect. It's worthwhile to review the minimum requirements, though, so that you don't run into difficulty trying to install it.

IBM PC or Compatible

You can use any of a variety of brands of PC, as long as the PC is an IBM or compatible. Check with your dealer if you're not sure if you have the right computer for WordPerfect.

Hard Drive

WordPerfect takes up more than 12 MB on your hard disk, so you should have at least a 40 MB hard drive to allow room for WordPerfect, the programs you create with it, and one or two other applications (if those other applications aren't too big.)

Floppy Drive

All computers come with at least one floppy disk drive, which usually takes either 5 1/4 inch disks or 3 1/2 inch disks. Be sure your installation disks are the same size as the drive on your computer.

Monochrome or Color Monitor

You can use either a monochrome or color monitor with WordPerfect. There are some advantages to working in color. You can readily distinguish among various kinds of highlighting on the screen, for instance. But you can do everything you need using a monochrome monitor, if that's what you have.

Keyboard and Mouse

Keyboards for PCs have become standard. Most use the AT style keyboard. You don't have to have a mouse, but WordPerfect 6.0 does offer certain shortcuts for mouse users, such as an optional button bar at the top of the screen for issuing certain commands.

Installing WordPerfect

You can't just copy the WordPerfect installation diskettes to your hard drive. You have to run the install program, which decompresses the files on the disks and puts them onto your hard drive:

1. Put the Install 1 disk in drive A.

2. At your computer's *C:* prompt, type `a:install`, and press Enter.

A screen comes up for you to tell WordPerfect whether you have a color monitor.

3. The programs asks, *Do you see red, green, and blue colored boxes?* If you see them, press y for Yes. Otherwise, press n.

4. Next, you choose from three types of installation—*Standard, Custom,* or *Network.* Press Enter to choose *Standard Installation* (see Figure A-1). Continue with Standard installation by pressing Enter to accept the suggested response in each case.

A window shows the directory where WordPerfect will be installed.

Press Enter to accept the suggested directory, *C:WP60.*

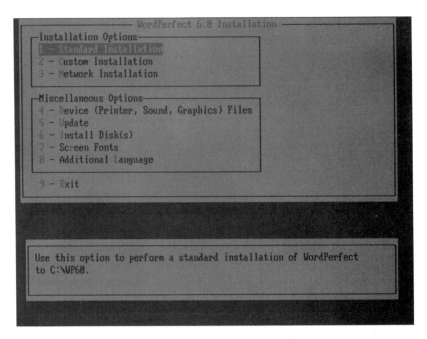

```
                    ───── WordPerfect 6.0 Installation ─────
  ┌Installation Options──────────────────────────┐
  │ 1 - Standard Installation                     │
  │ 2 - Custom Installation                       │
  │ 3 - Network Installation                      │
  │                                               │
  ┌Miscellaneous Options─────────────────────────┐
  │ 4 - Device (Printer, Sound, Graphics) Files   │
  │ 5 - Update                                    │
  │ 6 - Install Disk(s)                           │
  │ 7 - Screen Fonts                              │
  │ 8 - Additional Language                       │
  │                                               │
  │ 9 - Exit                                      │
  └───────────────────────────────────────────────┘



  ┌───────────────────────────────────────────────┐
  │ Use this option to perform a standard installation of WordPerfect │
  │ to C:\WP60.                                   │
  └───────────────────────────────────────────────┘
```

Figure A-1 Press Enter to accept Standard installation.

A window shows how much space there is available on your hard drive and shows you much you'll need for WordPerfect. If there's enough room, press Enter to continue with the installation.

Follow instructions on the screen for removing disks and inserting others.

Installing a Printer

To be able to print on your computer, WordPerfect has to know which printer you're using. At the end of installation, WordPerfect displays the *Printer Selection* window (see Figure A-2). If you want to install a printer later, after you've already installed WordPerfect, start installation as just described in *Installing WordPerfect,* but do this to install just a printer:

1. In the *WordPerfect 6.0 Installation* window (shown above, in Figure A-1), choose *Device (Printer, Sound, Graphics) Files* and continue to press Enter to accept the suggested responses.

2. In the *Install: Device* window, choose *Printer Files*. The Printer Selection window comes up.

Whether you're installing your printer during installation the first time, or later on, do this from the Printer Selection window.

1. Press n for *Name Search*.

2. In the *Name Search* window, begin typing the name of your printer.

3. When you've highlighted the name of your printer, press Enter, and press it again to confirm that you want to select the printer. Press Enter when asked if you want to install. WordPerfect installs the printer.

APPENDIX
B

WHICH KEYS DO I USE FOR
THAT AGAIN?

To find out many WordPerfect shortcut keys, just check the menus as you use them. If you find yourself doing something often, make mental note of the shortcut key from the menu, and begin to use it. Also, you can quickly look up the key combinations for various things by using Help:

1. Display the *Help* menu, and choose *Contents.*

2. From the *Help* window (see Figure B-1), you can see three different summaries of keystrokes:

For a list of what you can do with the Function keys—by themselves or combined with the Ctrl, Alt, or Shift keys—choose *Template* (see Figure B-2).

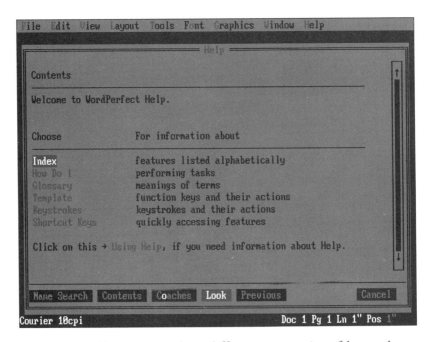

Figure B-1 You can get three different summaries of keystrokes from the Help menu.

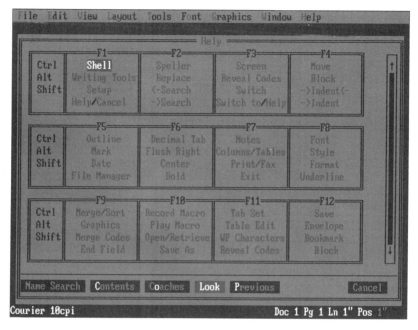

Figure B-2 The Template lists all the key combinations using Function keys.

For a summary of other key combinations, not using Function keys, choose *Keystrokes* (see Figure B-3).

For a summary of key combinations of Ctrl plus a letter key, choose *Shortcut Keys* (see Figure B-4).

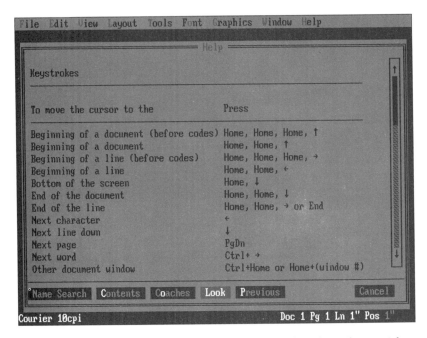

Figure B-3 Here's a summary of keystrokes other than those with Function keys or the Ctrl key.

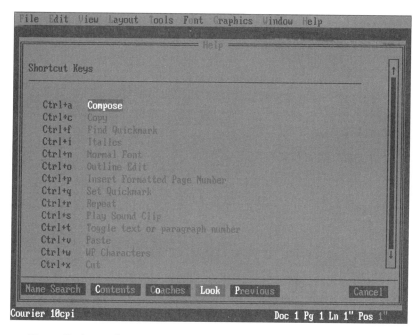

Figure B-4 For shortcuts, press Ctrl+a letter key.

INDEX

The book you hold in your hands
embodies a new concept in computer book publishing.
The cover and title page concepts were designed by award-winning designer
Christopher Johnson, who lives and works in New York city.
The interior book design by Carol Barth of Modern Design, in Los Angeles.
The interior text of the book was composed by Electric Ink Ltd. in
Penfield, New York, using QuarkXPress 3.1 on Apple Macintosh computers.
The body text is 11/13 Adobe Garamond.
The cover was designed on a Macintosh computer as well and uses
Franklin Gothic and Adobe Garamond typefaces.